SALVATION
IN CHRIST

SALVATION IN CHRIST

A Lutheran–Orthodox Dialogue

Edited and with an Introduction by
John Meyendorff
and Robert Tobias

Augsburg ■ Minneapolis

Library of Congress Cataloging-in-Publication Data

Salvation in Christ : a Lutheran–Orthodox dialogue / edited and with
   an introduction by John Meyendorff and Robert Tobias.
     p.   cm.
   Includes bibliographical references.
   ISBN 0-8066-2580-5 (alk. paper)
   1. Lutheran Church—Relations—Orthodox Eastern Church.
2. Orthodox Eastern Church—Relations—Lutheran Church. 3. Lutheran
Church—Doctrines. 4. Orthodox Eastern Church—Doctrines.
I. Meyendorff, John, 1926– . II. Tobias, Robert, 1919– .
BX324.52.S25   1992
234—dc20   91-42384
                                                   CIP

Manufactured in the U.S.A.   AF 9-2580

96   95   94   93   92   1   2   3   4   5   6   7   8   9   10

Contents

Foreword

Relationships and theological conversations between Lutherans and Orthodox have a history of almost five centuries. This story has some conspicuous gaps when contacts were few or misunderstandings were great. One of the fruits of the modern ecumenical movement is serious theological dialogue between divided Christians about precisely those matters of faith that keep them apart. Fortunately in recent decades on the world level, and in various countries and regions of the world, Lutherans and Orthodox have committed themselves to the intense work of dialogue, ever mindful that the unity they seek will finally be the gift of the Triune God whom they proclaim and worship.

It is especially appropriate that in the United States Lutheran–Orthodox dialogue has taken place. There are a number of similarities in the history of Lutherans and Orthodox in this country. Both have found settlement in the American scene challenging and rewarding. Both with strong roots elsewhere in the world have sought to contribute their witness to the Christian faith in a new land. Both brought histories and traditions into a new context that has presented them with fresh opportunities and concerns.

Since the early 1960s there have been three occasions for Lutherans and Orthodox to engage in dialogue together, the most recent being between 1983 and 1989. This last series of dialogues sponsored by the Standing Conference of the Canonical Orthodox Bishops in the Americas, the Evangelical Lutheran Church in America and the Lutheran Church–Missouri Synod concentrated on the significant theological topics of divinization and justification. Included in the volume are the final report *Christ in Us and Christ for Us* and a number of supporting papers.

We urge the members of our churches, the clergy and the faithful, to study this material prayerfully and carefully. It shows how much Lutherans and Orthodox can say together about crucial topics of the Christian faith and indicates hope for the future of our ecumenical work together.

His Eminence Archbishop Iakovos, Primate
Greek Orthodox Archdiocese of North and South America

The Rev. Herbert W. Chilstrom, Bishop
Evangelical Lutheran Church in America

Introduction

Let us undertake conversations . . . with a view to creating a broader base of understanding in the hope that a tangible and enduring bond of unity may be achieved.[1]

The 16th century correspondence between the Tübingen (Lutheran) theologians and (Orthodox) Patriarch Jeremias II is "unfinished business." We should move on from there with studies of the Nicene Creed, the Councils, and the Augsburg Confession, and especially with the doctrine of the Church.[2]

Such were the expectations of our Lutheran and Orthodox leaders that led to the beginnings of dialogue in North America in 1965. It was time to examine our roots and possibilities for rapprochement.

BACKGROUND IN AMERICA

In 1767 Greek Orthodox refugees from Asia Minor were brought to Florida to cultivate indigo. Russian Orthodox missionaries arrived in Alaska in 1794, established schools, a seminary, and provided Scriptures and liturgy in the native language. A diocese was established in 1840 and after 1880 the mission was extended to both California and the east coast, when masses of immigrants arrived. Scandinavian ancestors of Lutheran immigrants had established colonies on the eastern seaboard nearly five hundred years before America's "discovery" by Columbus in 1492, but these colonies had disappeared by the time Lutherans began arriving in the late 1600s. So our eighteenth- and nineteenth-century ancestors arriving on the east coast, mostly lay people, entered a strange new land on their own. Most of the settlers they found here were English-speaking; were religiously Puritan, Calvinist, or Unitarian; had a separated church and state; had no king or princes; and had few if any clergy of their own. But the Orthodox and Lutherans had then and have now some fundamental religious commitments which held steady and eventually inclined us toward one another.

It was not so at first. Until this generation there was little religious contact between Orthodox and Lutherans, for several reasons. (1) Lutheran immigration (after a small influx of forty thousand around 1700) took place in the mid-1800s (four million). Several hundred thousand Orthodox immigrants arrived later, after Lutherans were regarded as established "Americans." (2) Lutheran immigrants settled predominantly in farm areas and pursued farm-related occupations; the Orthodox, however, went into urban marketing and mining. (3) Orthodox spoke and wrote in Greek, Russian, Serbian, Arabic, Bulgarian, Romanian; Lutherans spoke and wrote in German and Scandinavian languages plus some twenty-five other languages and dialects. Contact between groups was therefore limited. There are some recorded instances of warm hospitality extended to Orthodox by Lutherans and vice versa; but among laity in frontier situations where much was already strange, there was also suspicion about the "strange" customs of one another.

It was not until the second and third quarters of this century that suspicion and exclusion were transformed into concern, appreciation, and inquiry. Today, the millions of Lutherans and Orthodox who once were separated not only by faith, but also by different cultural, ethnic, and linguistic backgrounds are sharing the same North American culture, speaking the same language, with their youth being educated in the same schools and united by the same cultural interests. This places both groups in a better position than their forebears have ever been to understand that which still separates them and to work for unity in faith.

OFFICIAL DIALOGUES, ROUND 1

If our official conversations in North America were sparked by the Lord of the one church, they have been kindled by the tragic and heroic events of World War II. Central figures in our dialogue shared experiences of those events. They are the ones who initiated the first round of dialogues in 1965: His Eminence Archbishop Iakovos for the Standing Conference of Canonical Orthodox Bishops in the Americas and Dr. Paul Empie for the USA National Committee of the Lutheran World Federation. The subject proposed for the first session, held in 1967, was "The Nature of the Church." As the date approached, the subject was changed to "Lutheran and Orthodox Churches in (American) Perspective," and "Scripture and Tradition." In a concluding press release the dialogue declared:

> Presentations on the contemporary life of the two church traditions not only furthered mutual understanding of respective relationships and activities but also revealed, somewhat unexpectedly, a number of parallel situations and problems faced by these groups in the course of their history in this country . . .
>
> In discussing the subject of "Scripture and Tradition," it quickly became evident that for both groups these two terms do not denote elements in the Christian faith which stand apart from and in contrast to each other, but rather are inseparably related.

The second session was held in 1969. Again, "striking parallels" were noted in the growth of each church in America; emphasis of both on the liturgy, the key role of the celebrant in the Eucharist, the importance of creedal and confessional statements, the gradual centralization of authority in American Lutheranism and the *de facto* congregational character of Orthodoxy in America. Major attention was given to the relation of Scripture and Tradition. Issues were identified and clarified, particularly the question of authority. The interrelating of Scripture and Tradition was again recognized, although further work was assumed to be needed on this issue. Still, sufficient agreement was reached, together with the later work of Lutheran–Orthodox bilaterals abroad, to indicate that we may not need to take this up as a major concern.

Other significant findings were recorded from these two brief sessions: participants recognized that there was something very special, if not unique, in their situation as immigrant churches in this new land, especially the overlayering of different national roots and ecclesial judicatories, contrary to the one-church-in-one-place ecclesiology of both; and the critical function of liturgy in theological work and the unifying process.

Below these common problems, the two partners were both solidly Trinitarian and shared a common ultimate concern for continuity, for "real and living presence," for the participation of the "earthy" in sacred acts. From that both were sacramental, mystical, and liturgical.

By 1970, demands upon Orthodox representatives to participate in numerous bilateral dialogues were too many for the small number of Orthodox theologians available at that time. The Reformed-Orthodox and Lutheran-Orthodox bilaterals were merged into a Reformed–Lutheran–Orthodox trilateral. The subject matter at that point shifted from strictly doctrinal issues to social responsibility. After three sessions delegates reported "new friendships, deepened understanding, freedom from necessity for ecclesial rapprochement, and freedom from the adversarial spirit associated with bilateral dialogue." But the issues and affirmations common to Lutherans and Orthodox had yet to be attended to.

OFFICIAL DIALOGUES, ROUND 2

The second round of dialogues began with an introductory meeting in New York, December 13–14, 1983. Papers were read on the general background of Lutheran–Orthodox relationships in Europe and America, and on the Jeremias–Tübingen correspondence in the sixteenth century.[3] It was decided that the next stage of work was to examine the seven "Great Councils": do we affirm them today, with or without reservations, as common ground? After the first session we agreed to focus this round's major efforts on the subject of salvation. However, the first two sessions of the dialogue did some groundwork and produced some preliminary observations on unity, councils, creeds/confessions and *filioque* which we note briefly here for reflection and future reference.

An early task was to review our respective visions of unity and identify common ground from which we could proceed.[4] It is the ultimate hope of those who initiated this dialogue and of participant members to arrive at a shared life in one church: a common faith, sacramental celebration, ministry, witness—in short, full communion in one church with whatever regional governances and ethnic customs. Toward that end both Lutherans and Orthodox hold that common agreement must be found in essential teachings of the faith for the sharing of a common and complete Eucharistic life. This does not imply uniformity of worship and traditions. Nor is one expected to abandon his or her tradition and merge or be converted to the other. But in the struggle for truth and wholeness all should strive in their own churches and traditions to deepen the fullness of the apostolic faith embodied in a fully ecclesial life,[5] until both Orthodox and Lutherans arrive at mutual affirmation in apostolic continuity and common participation in the mystery of the church. In the ecumenical debate—which comes first, reconciling diversities or developing a shared life?—we recognize what may be a unique possibility in America where we have the necessary scholars and congregations in neighboring proximity to proceed simultaneously with unity in doctrinal commitment and a shared life. This will take some special working materials, some leadership preparation among students, clergy, and laity; we offer the *Handbook* supplement to this report as a beginning step.

At its first session the dialogue also recognized a large measure of common understanding in our perception of the nature and meaning of councils.[6] In Councils the church maintains the visible consensus and coherence of the church across time and space, the common witness of each local church in the fullness of the whole, and the whole church in life of each local church. In Councils the church manifests particular aspects for its life (worship, oneness, continuity of living tradition, theological articulation, order); other aspects of the life of the church are manifest in church schools, congregational gatherings, monastic life, and hospitals; but all are part of each, of the church, the same church. In Councils, as also in local worship, we are "contemporaries of the fathers," participating in the continuation of the *consensus fidelium et patrum*, the same living and continuous faith of the church, the same church. In responding to heresies, Councils of the church, under the guidance of the Holy Spirit, articulate the unanimous, catholic, Christian faith and confessions of the orthodox and true church, given once and for all to the saints. There are, however, serious questions that will still need clarification: the membership of councils; whether and in what ways Councils or pre-Councils can express the full unity of the church; and beyond that, what is the fullness of the church.

Our second session (December 1985) began with consideration of creeds and confessions.[7] Against anti-credalists we agree that the church has the responsibility to articulate the faith in the clearest possible terminology, while recognizing that the words, phrases, and definitions of creed and confession cannot exhaust or fully describe the mysteries of the faith or of the total life of the church.

In the face of such mysteries, of paradox and vastness in divine self-revelation, such articulations have a witnessing, corrective, and liturgical function. They serve as descriptions, as checkpoints, out of the living consciousness of the church in which the content and spirit of Scriptures and holy Tradition have been tested and are embodied. They witness to and clarify true faith. The Nicene-Constantinopolitan Creed, in the context of continuing Councils, serves in a normative way in disclosing and proclaiming who the triune God is. Since this primary Creed of all Christendom, confessions in several forms have appeared in both Lutheran and Orthodox communities to interpret and clarify the faith in new situations or to correct questionable belief or practices. The Nicene Creed, however, is the one Creed that takes precedence over local or regional confessions for both Lutherans and Orthodox. Generally, the Orthodox attribute less importance to such "confessional" texts than the Lutherans, and they insist on the wholeness of Tradition expressed in worship and continuity of teaching.

Our discussion of the *filioque*,[8] the interpretation added to the Nicene-Constantinopolitan Creed by the Western church that the Holy Spirit proceeds from the Father "and the Son," is unfinished. But the work already done alongside that of other Lutheran–Orthodox dialogues and the larger ecumenical dialogue leads us to recommend that materials be prepared in English for serious study in all our parishes on the being and action of the Holy Spirit in light of recent ecumenical research, while preserving the use of the Creed in its original form, without *filioque*. For some Lutherans the latter is already possible and desirable, for others it is not. For all Orthodox, the Creed is used in its original, unaltered form.

The second session of the dialogue also launched us into the study of salvation, and subsequent sessions pushed us more deeply into the issues of justification, *theosis*, sanctification, free will, election, predestination, and eschatology under the general heading, "Salvation as communion with God." Under this heading, the central focus has not been so much on the "how" of salvation as on the "content" of salvation. Our findings, agreements and disagreements, convergences and divergences, and recommendations are reported in the Agreed Statement which follows. In most cases major papers on the subject, as those in volume 2, have been somewhat revised and condensed by the authors after discussion with the Dialogue, and are commended to readers for careful study and response.

John Meyendorff   Robert Tobias
Orthodox Auxiliary Co-Chair   Lutheran Auxiliary Co-Chair

COMMON STATEMENT

Christ "In Us" and Christ "For Us" in Lutheran and Orthodox Theology

Introduction

According to an ancient tradition of the church, the task of theology is to express what is "befitting God" (*theoprepes*). Seldom has this meant coining new words. The primary vehicle of theology has always been the language of the Bible. Even in the most sophisticated theological debates, for example in the disputes over the person of Christ in the fifth century, theologians seldom strayed far from the words and images of the Holy Scriptures. On occasion, non-biblical terms were employed in dogmatic formulation, e.g., *homoousios* (of one essence) in the creed adopted at the Council of Nicaea in A.D. 325, or the four adverbs in the decree of the Council of Chalcedon in A.D. 451, "without confusion, without change, without division, without separation." But these non-biblical terms were always surrounded by biblical words and expressions and were understood within the context of the Scriptures. To this day, as is evident in terms such as grace, justification, sanctification, faith, redemption, salvation, and image of God, the native tongue of Christians, for the theological expression as well as for speaking of the Christian life, is the language of the Bible.

The language of the Scriptures is, however, not univocal,and in the course of time biblical terms took on new connotations or overtones (sometimes assuming a life of their own), as they were filtered through Christian experience and thought. For that reason, even though Lutherans and Orthodox read the same Scriptures and share a common spiritual and theological heritage derived from the early church, our different historical experiences have led us to accentuate distinctive features of the biblical tradition. In piety, liturgy, and theology, Lutherans have their roots in the Western Catholic tradition that developed independently of the East for a thousand years before the Reformation. The Eastern Catholic tradition has its roots in Byzantium, the Middle East and the Slavic world. Though Eastern and Western Christians share a common heritage in the Scriptures, the church fathers, and the early ecumenical councils, they have had little contact with each other for more than a thousand years. After the seventh century and the rise of Islam, Orthodoxy was isolated from the west and large sections of Eastern Christianity were destined to exist for centuries under Muslim and Mongol hegemony and later under Ottoman rule—all hostile in varying degrees to Christianity. These historical, cultural, and political experiences have formed the Orthodox churches in ways that are difficult for Western Christians to comprehend. Conversely, the Orthodox have had no firsthand experience with the distinctive religious and theological concerns of the Reformation, an event that took place only in Western Christendom, and one which is formative for the theological and spiritual outlook of the churches of the Augsburg Confession.

In our discussions over the last six years we have had less difficulty understanding each other when we speak of the principal dogmas formulated by the early church, e.g., the doctrine of the Holy Trinity or the doctrine of Christ, than we have when discussing the mystery of salvation and the particulars of the spiritual life. This report highlights some of the difficulties Lutherans and Orthodox encounter as we try to understand each other on the topic of salvation in Christ and some of the areas in which we have found convergence and agreement. We are not ready to say, as Saint Cyril of Alexandria said in A.D. 433, in a letter announcing theological agreement with Bishop John of Antioch, "Let the heavens rejoice and the earth be glad, for the middle wall of partition is broken down."[1] But we are happy to report that the obstacles to understanding seem less formidable than they did when we began to talk to one another six years ago.

In our traditions, differences of understanding have arisen with respect to a number of terms and phrases: "justification and sanctification," *theosis* (deification), "imputed righteousness," "image of God," "free will," "synergism," "sharing the divine nature," "nature," "grace," "sin," "original sin," and other expressions that bear on the Christian understanding of salvation.

18

JUSTIFICATION AND SANCTIFICATION

In the sixteenth century, when the first tentative contacts took place between the reformers and the patriarchs of Constantinople, language was a barrier. It was not that the reformers did not know Greek (Philipp Melanchthon, for example, was a distinguished humanist), but that biblical terms had come to assume different meanings for the two traditions. The term "justify" in the Augsburg Confession was on one occasion translated by "sanctify" in the version sent to the patriarch of Constantinople, Jeremiah II.[2] Of course Orthodox and Lutherans alike, following the Scripture, used the two terms, but each tradition was heir to a different theological heritage, the one shaped by the scholastic debates of medieval Western theology, the other by the theological developments within the churches of the Eastern Christian and Byzantine world.

For the Lutherans "justification" and "sanctification" are two distinct theological categories, one designating God's declaration of righteousness, the other the gradual process of growth in the Christian life. Hence Lutherans interpret the term "justify" by means of texts such as Rom. 3:23-24, "Since all have sinned and fall short of the glory of God, they are now justified by his grace as a gift, through the redemption that is in Christ Jesus." The Orthodox believe that "justification" initiates a change in human beings and begins the process of growth in the Christian life (what Lutherans call "sanctification"). Furthermore, the Orthodox understand "justification" as forgiveness of sins and deliverance from death, and "sanctification" as spiritual growth, which is related to the work of the Holy Spirit in us.[3] Hence they see "justification" and "sanctification" as one divine action, as Saint Paul writes in 1 Cor. 6:11: "You were washed, you were sanctified, you were justified in the name of the Lord Jesus Christ and in the Spirit of our God." It is easy to understand why "justify" could be translated "sanctify" from the perspective of the Orthodox, yet such a translation confounded the Lutheran view of justification.

THEOSIS (DEIFICATION)

For the Orthodox *theosis* is a central theological and religious idea, as the title of the book by Georgios I. Mantzaridis, *The Deification of Man*, indicates. "In the Orthodox understanding Christianity signifies not merely an adherence to certain dogmas, not merely an exterior imitation of Christ through moral effort, but *direct union* with the living God, the total transformation of the human person by divine grace and glory—what the Greek fathers termed 'deification' . . . (*theosis*)," writes Bishop Kallistos Ware.[4] Although the term *theosis* does not occur in the Holy Scriptures, the idea of sharing in the divine nature (which *theosis* means) does occur. The locus classicus is 2 Pet. 1:3-4: "His divine power has given us everything needed for life and godliness, through the knowledge of him who called us by his own glory and goodness. Thus he has given us, through these things, his precious and very great promises, so that through them you may escape from the corruption that is in the world because of lust, and may become participants of the divine nature." Although 2 Peter uses the term "divine nature," in this passage, according to the Orthodox, it should not be understood to refer to the transcendent divine being (*ousia*), which is incommunicable; here the word nature refers to the communicable attributes of God, the divine energies.[5]

Of course the passage in 2 Peter is not the only place where the idea of deification is expressed in the Scriptures. Similar concepts appear elsewhere. "Beloved, we are God's children now; what we will be has not yet been revealed. What we do know is this: when he is revealed we will be like him . . ." (1 John 3:2). But the passage in 2 Peter is the most explicit statement within the New Testament and it delineates the central feature of the Orthodox conception. Salvation is understood to mean "participation" or "sharing" or "fellowship" with God, or "indwelling" in the words of the Gospel of John. "You know him, because he abides with you, and he will be in you" (John 14:17). As Vladimir Lossky writes:

> Thus the redeeming work of Christ . . . is seen to be directly related to the ultimate goal of creatures: to know union with God. If this union has been accomplished in the divine person of the Son, who is God become man, it is necessary that each human person, in turn, should become god by grace, or "a partaker of the divine nature," according to Saint Peter's expression.[6]

Deification does not mean that human beings "become God" in a pantheistic sense. Believers enter into a personal relationship with God through Baptism and participate fully in God's life through the sacraments in the church, the body of Christ, [and] the community of the people of God.

2 Peter 1:4 has no such importance in Lutheran thinking or spirituality. Lutherans are more inclined to cite 1 Pet. 2:24 than 2

Peter: "He himself bore our sins in his body on the cross, so that, free from sins, we might die to sin and live for righteousness." Or 1 Peter 3:18: "For Christ also died for sins once for all, the righteous for the unrighteous, that he might bring us to God. . . ." In speaking of salvation, Lutherans have emphasized the language of vicarious atonement, imputation, and forensic justification, rather than the language of participation or communion. Justification is that act by which God removes the sentence of condemnation on human beings, releases them from guilt, and ascribes to them the merit of Christ. Lutherans have more often spoken of Christ "for us" than they have of Christ "in us." In his commentary of Gal. 3:13, Martin Luther wrote: "Christ is a divine and human Person who took sin, the condemnation of the law, and death upon Himself, not for Himself but for us. Therefore the whole emphasis is on the phrase 'for us.' "[7] In the Apology to the Augsburg Confession Philipp Melanchthon said that "the gospel is, strictly speaking, the promise of forgiveness of sins and justification *because of Christ*."[8]

Yet, "Christ for us" was never a rigid scheme within the Lutheran tradition. Occasionally salvation was expressed in the language of union or even as "sharing in the divine nature," especially in sermons and devotional literature. In his sermons on 2 Peter, for example, Luther said that "through the power of faith . . . we partake of and have association or communion with the divine nature." He observes, however, that the language of 2 Pet. 1:4 is "without parallel in the New and the Old Testament." Nevertheless, finding it in harmony with the rest of the Scripture, he says:

> What is the divine nature? It is . . . eternal truth, righteousness, wisdom, everlasting life, peace, joy, happiness, and whatever can be called good. Now he [or she] who becomes a partaker of the divine nature receives all this, so that he [or she] lives eternally and has everlasting peace, joy and happiness, and is pure, clean, righteous, almighty against the devil, sin, and death.[9]

Martin Luther's interpretation of this passage from 2 Peter is echoed in an important devotional book written by a Lutheran pastor early in the seventeenth century. This is Johann Arndt's *True Christianity*, a work that was read widely by Lutherans until early in this century. Arndt writes:

> By this deep trust and heartfelt assent, a man [or woman] gives his [or her] heart completely and utterly to God, rests in God

alone, gives himself [herself] over to God, clings to God alone, unites himself [herself] with God, is a participant of all that which is God and Christ, becomes one spirit with God, receives from God new power, new life, new consolation, peace and joy, rest of soul, righteousness and holiness, and also, from God through faith, one is reborn. [p. 45].

Arndt also speaks of salvation as communion with God.

Since Christ now lives and dwells in you through faith, his indwelling is not a dead work but a living work. As a result, renewal from Christ through faith comes about.

Grace brings about two things in you: first, faith places Christ in you and makes you his possession; second, it renews you in Christ so that you grow, blossom, and live in him. What is the use of a graft in a stem if it does not grow and bring forth fruit? . . . The true sanctifying faith renews the whole person, purifies the heart, unites with God (p. 47). . . .[10]

Furthermore, salvation as sharing in the divine nature is also affirmed in the Formula of Concord. The discussion there centers on matters of Christology, specifically the hypostatic union of the divine and human natures in Christ. The authors of the Formula of Concord draw a parallel between the union of Christ and the believer and the union of the two natures in Christ: "Saint Peter testifies with clear words that even we, in whom Christ dwells only by grace, have in Christ, because of this exalted mystery, become 'partakers of the divine nature.' "[11] If this is so, continues the Formula of Concord, how much more intimate must be the union of God and human beings in Christ when the apostle says, "in him [Christ] the whole fullness of deity dwells bodily" (Col. 2:9).

What can we conclude from this brief discussion of *theosis* and related theological ideas? The term "deification" is commonly employed among Orthodox, but not among Lutherans, and does not have wide currency in Western theology.[12] The Orthodox understanding of "deification," which was developed most fully in the patristic period, however, has its roots in the Scripture passages in 2 Peter and 1 John, in the images in the Gospel of John that speak of union between Christ and the believer (e.g., the vine and the branches), and in the concept of mutual indwelling (John 1:32; 14:17, et al.). Similarly, Saint Paul says in Gal. 2:20: "It is no longer I who live but it is Christ who lives in me." These biblical expressions build a bridge across the divide that separates us. The Orthodox understand salvation as communion with God and sharing in God's life in the fellowship of the church, the body of Christ, and the temple of the Holy Spirit. These theological expressions are biblical so they also appear from time to time in Lutheran writings, but without the same centrality and degree of consistency. Although Lutherans are wary to speak of the "deification" of human beings, they do speak of "giving one's heart wholly to God," or "clinging to God alone," and of the "union of God and human beings in Christ." And they affirm that communion with God is mediated through the Word and Sacraments within the fellowship of the church.

In the Lutheran understanding, justification is God's gracious declaration of forgiveness. This justifying word comes to the sinner from without by a declaration of God, by imputation. There is no place for human cooperation in justification; it is God's work alone. Justification, however, requires faith, for it is through faith that believers make Christ's redemptive death and resurrection their own. Faith lays hold of God's action in Christ. Abraham believed God, "Therefore his faith 'was reckoned to him as righteousness' " (Rom. 4:22).

In the dialogues between Lutherans and Orthodox in Finland, it was stated that "faith" played a role in Lutheran theology similar to the role of "*theosis*" in Orthodox theology. *In ipsa fide Christus adest.* (In faith itself Christ is present.) Faith is a way of speaking about union between the believer and God, about fellowship with God. Saint Gregory of Nyssa wrote: From the history of Abraham we learn that one cannot "draw near to God unless faith mediates and unites the soul that seeks God to that [divine] nature that is beyond our comprehension."[13] To become "sons and daughters of God" is to enter into intimate communion with God through the Spirit who dwells in us, a union that is nurtured by the Word and Sacraments within the fellowship of the church. The Finnish statement reads:

> It was perceived that aspects of soteriology are not unrelated to each other nor contradictory, but the traditional Lutheran doctrine of justification contains the idea of the deification of [human beings]. Justification and deification are based on the real presence of Christ in the word of God, in the sacraments, and in worship.[14]

The term *theosis*, what appears to be a major point of contention between Lutherans and Orthodox, can be seen as a fruitful point of convergence from another perspective. The teaching about deification expresses a profound biblical truth that the two traditions share. Both Lutherans and Orthodox affirm that the ultimate goal of salvation is communion with the living God. Reconciliation and fellowship with God is made possible only through the act of divine grace in Christ's vicarious death and resurrection. By the initiative that belongs wholly to the triune God, human beings are introduced into a personal relationship of participation in God's life. By grace we share in what God is by nature and become what God intended us to be.

There are differences in the way the two traditions understand righteousness. Both Lutherans and Orthodox insist that sinners are forgiven without any merit of their own; the only merit is the cross of Christ. Whereas the Orthodox see righteousness as the inner transformation toward "God-likeness" (i.e., sanctification in Lutheran terminology), Lutherans say that righteousness is imputed to humans. But on the fundamental point, that salvation is a gratuitous act by which God draws sinners into a loving relationship with himself, there is no disagreement. In our view one reason for this is that both traditions have continued to employ the language of the Bible as the primary vehicle of theological expression and spiritual understanding.

REDEMPTION AND TRIUMPH OVER DEATH

Just as the reformers were capable of using the idea of "partaking of the divine nature" and not simply the model of vicarious atonement to speak of salvation, so the Orthodox, following the Scriptures, also speak of the vicarious death of Christ, Christ "for us" (*pro nobis*), and affirm the necessity of the sacrificial work of Christ. They insist, however, that the "juridical image of Redemption" must be completed by the "physical image of the triumph over death . . ."[15] but they do not rule out the Western church's way of conceiving redemption. Nor did the early fathers express the mystery of salvation in only one image. Saint Athanasius writes:

> But since the debt owed by all men had still to be paid, since all . . . had to die, therefore after the proof of his divinity given by his works, he now on behalf of all men offered the sacrifice and surrendered his own temple to death on behalf of all, in order to make them all guiltless and free from the first transgression, and to reveal himself superior to death, showing his

24

own incorruptible body as first-fruits of the universal resurrection.[16]

Yet, as John Meyendorff observes, the Anselmian idea of "satisfaction" is not commonplace in Orthodoxy. "Byzantine theology did not produce any significant elaboration of the Pauline doctrine of justification expressed in Romans and Galatians. The Greek patristic commentaries on such passages as Gal. 3:13 ("Christ redeemed us from the curse of the law by becoming a curse for us") generally interpret the idea of redemption by substitution in the wider context of victory over death and of sanctification."[17] Lutherans also speak of redemption in terms of Christ's victory over death.

It was a strange and dreadful strife
When life and death contended;
The victory remained with life,
The reign of death was ended.
Holy Scripture plainly says
That death is swallowed up by death,
Its sting is lost forever.[18]

Nevertheless, here too there is a significant difference of emphasis. Just as Lutherans have been uncomfortable with the idea of "deification," so the Orthodox have been uneasy with medieval Western formulations that conceive of Christ's atonement as a "satisfaction" for sins. How one assesses these differences depends, in large measure, on how much weight one gives to a specific view of atonement. There is no question that Lutherans and Orthodox are drawn to different biblical words and images to express their respective understanding of salvation. Put much too simply, Lutherans emphasize Galatians and Romans, Orthodox emphasize the Gospel of John and First John. What divides us has less to do with the doctrinal heritage of the early church (e.g., the creed of Nicaea, or the christological statement of faith of the Council of Chalcedon), than with the way the two traditions have appropriated different aspects of the Scriptures in preaching and teaching salvation.

THE IMAGE OF GOD

Lutherans and Orthodox make different use of the biblical phrase "image of God." For the Orthodox the image of God is the "great

25

natural prerogative" of human beings, and refers to specific characteristics in them, notably free will and rationality. Saint Gregory of Nyssa writes: "There is in us the possibility for everything good, for all virtue and wisdom, and every better thing that can be conceived; but one thing is preeminent among all, that we are free from necessity, and are not subject to any natural power, but have within ourselves the power to choose what we wish."[19] Saint Gregory's reasoning is that human beings are moral creatures and that virtue would have no meaning if human beings were not free. Furthermore, the Eastern church fathers see the image of God in human beings as a reflection of divine life and especially divine love, in which human beings were called to grow in likeness with God. The failure of human beings to grow in likeness to God deprived them of authentic life, which is impossible without God. However, for the Orthodox at the fall the image of God was tarnished, but not effaced. Lutherans tend to say that in the fall the image of God was "effaced" or "lost." Nevertheless, Lutheran theology has long recognized the distinction between broad and narrow senses of the image of God.

A key to understanding the use of the image of God in the two traditions can be found in different understandings of the scriptural use of the term. One use is found in the locus classicus in Gen. 1:26: "Then God said, 'Let us make humankind in our image, according to our likeness. . . .' " As Saint Gregory (and almost all Christian theologians) understands the passage from Genesis, "image of God" designates those unique gifts that God bestowed on human beings: free will, rationality, speech, and the capacity for communion with God. The other is found in the New Testament texts that speak of the restoration of the image in Christ (such as Col. 1:15; 3:10, and Eph. 5:9), which speak of putting on a new nature "which is being renewed in knowledge according to the image of its creator." Both understandings of the "image of God" can be found in the early fathers. We have already cited Saint Gregory of Nyssa on one sense of the term. A text attributed to his older brother, Saint Basil of Caesarea, uses image of God in its christological sense.

> Human beings were created according to the image and likeness of God, but sin deformed the beauty of the image, drawing the soul to passionate desires. But God, who made human beings, is the true life. Whoever has lost the likeness to God, lost fellowship with the light; whatever is without God is not

able to share in the blessed light. Let us therefore return to the grace which we possessed from the beginning to which we have become strangers through sin.[20]

In general, Lutherans prefer to speak of the image of God in its christological sense to designate that which was lost in the fall and regained in redemption; Orthodox prefer to speak of the image of God as those distinctively divine qualities reflected in human beings, free will and rationality, which continue to be part of human nature after the fall. However, the Orthodox often make further distinctions between image and likeness (Gen. 1:26). What was lost at the fall was the "likeness" of God, "fellowship with the light," and "communion with God through love." Christ restored this "fallen" image by regaining for us that which we had at the beginning, indeed more than what was bound in Adam; through his incarnation, death, and resurrection Christ once and for all achieved life in communion with God. Neither view, however, excludes the other.

Lutherans believe that human beings retain a basic knowledge of right and wrong, the use of reason in matters of justice, and some sense of God's existence through natural knowledge. As the Lutheran theologian John Gerhard expressed it, everything depends on how one defines the image of God. If the image is only understood to be the essence of the soul, intellect, will, and other "natural prerogatives," it is not lost through the fall. If, however, the image of God is also understood to mean "righteousness and true holiness," then the image of God has been lost in the fall and regained in Christ. Furthermore, what is regained is in Christ more wonderful than what was lost: "By the grace of Christ and the Holy Spirit, that image of God into which we have begun to be remade in this life, will one day shine in us more brightly and more gloriously than it once shone in Adam, for he was able not to die, but we are not able to die."[21]

NATURE AND GRACE

Like the term "deification" and the phrase "image of God," the terms "nature" and "grace" carry different overtones within Lutheran and Orthodox traditions. Some Lutherans, for example, could say, "we are by nature sinful and unclean," a formulation that Orthodox would not normally employ. On occasion, however, the Eastern Orthodox fathers depict sin in language that is no less

27

vivid than that of the Lutheran reformers. Saint Gregory of Nyssa wrote:

> Because of the guile of him who sowed in us the weeds of disobedience, our nature no longer preserves the stamp of the divine image; it has been transformed and made ugly by sin. Freely our nature chose to act in accord with the evil one. For this reason human nature has become a member of the evil family of the father of sin.[22]

Lutheran theology has never asserted that human beings are "by nature" sinful. If they are, there could be no redemption. The term "nature" in the phrase "by nature sinful" is a metaphorical expression to express the corrupting power of sin in the lives of human beings. The Lutheran position is more clearly expressed in statements such as:

> We believe, teach, and confess that there is a distinction between human nature and original sin, not only in the beginning when God created human beings pure and holy and without sin, but also as we now have our nature after the Fall. Even after the Fall our nature is and remains a creation of God. The distinction between our nature and original sin is as great as the difference between God's Work and the devil's work.[23]

The Orthodox speak of sin as "fallenness." Humanity strayed from the path of communion with God and now finds itself in a "fallen state." This state is defined in terms of morality (since there is no authentic life apart from God) and distorted priorities, not by expressions such as "natural corruption" or "inherited guilt" as among Lutherans. Sin, which is living out of communion with God, is the lack of true humanness. Therefore it is said that the image of God, the sign of true humanness, has been tarnished. For this reason Christ could become fully human yet remain without sin. In the fallen state human beings are dominated by the "flesh" which, instead of leading nature toward God and to communion with him, turns it away from God.

FREE WILL

Lutherans believe that human beings were created good, and that the fall into sin did not destroy the possibility for this goodness to be restored. Yet they embrace a more pessimistic view of human beings than the Orthodox. Lutherans do not speak of "synergy" (cooperation with God) with respect to justification. "Free will," then, is another concept that has different connotations for Lutherans and Orthodox. In an early treatise Martin Luther wrote: "After the fall of Adam, free will is a mere expression; whenever it acts in character, it commits mortal sin."[24] Not all of Luther's utterances are normative for Lutherans, yet statements such as this, and the experience that underlies it, have shaped Lutheran attitudes toward nature, grace, and free will.

In the case of "free will" it is apparent that different historical experiences and different memories have shaped Orthodox and Lutheran views. Early Christian debates with pagan philosophers over "free will" still inform Orthodox thinking; Lutherans bring a distinctly medieval, Western agenda to the discussion. In the ancient world, freedom of choice (freedom of the will) was seen as a necessary doctrine if there was to be any sense of moral responsibility. How could it be said that one was responsible for one's action, i.e., that moral acts were possible, unless one could "choose" one course over another? Without freedom of the will all human actions are determined by external causes. For this reason "free will" became a foundational teaching of the Christian church and was affirmed by all the early fathers, East and West, including Saint Augustine, especially in his earlier writings.[25]

For the Orthodox the teaching on free will has not led to the belief that humans can save themselves by their own works or efforts. This is what has been referred to as the Pelagian error that the church repudiated in the fifth and sixth centuries. On the contrary, free will was a way of asserting human freedom, and the possibility of fellowship with God and love, for "where there is no freedom there can be no love."[26] Saint Paul says: "Work out your own salvation with fear and trembling; for it is God who is at work in you, enabling you both to will and to work for his good pleasure" (Phil. 2:12-13). In the Orthodox view there can be no contradiction between grace and free will, or between nature and grace. As John Chrysostom wrote: "Human will is not sufficient, unless one receives aid from above; on the other hand we gain nothing by aid from above if there is no willingness."[27] No one has a "natural power" to earn salvation, yet God allows humans to cooperate with grace to embark on the path toward fellowship with God (*theosis*). Fellowship with God does not mean participation in the divine essence (*ousia*) but in the divine attributes or qualities (energies) that God shares with human beings.

On this point the differences between the Lutherans and the Orthodox are noteworthy. Each affirms the "freedom of the will" but restricts the arena in which the will is active. Here the Lutheran distinction between "justification" and "sanctification" must be kept in mind. In justification the will is powerless and cannot cooperate with God's grace. "For this reason the mind that is set on the flesh is hostile to God; it does not submit to God's laws—indeed it cannot, and those who are in the flesh cannot please God" (Rom. 8:7). After regeneration, however, the will of the believer, nourished by the Word and Sacraments, learns to desire the good and to work with the Holy Spirit in achieving holiness. Once liberated by "God's power and activity," the human will "becomes an instrument and means of God the Holy Spirit, so that human beings not only lay hold on grace but also cooperate with the Holy Spirit in the works that follow."[28]

We do not wish to minimize our differences on this matter, but it may be helpful to observe on this question, as on others, that the way the two traditions have appropriated the Scriptures has shaped the way that they have understood the mystery of salvation and sanctification. The Orthodox think of one continuous process, whereas the Lutherans distinguish the initial act of justification and regeneration from the process of sanctification. As we have already observed, the different emphases can be traced back to different biblical metaphors. If the metaphor for salvation is communion or participation, then it is natural and inevitable that one speaks of cooperation, of willing, and of love as ways in which fellowship with God is deepened and strengthened. Many texts from the Scriptures speak of salvation in these terms. If, however, the primary biblical metaphor is that of a vicarious death, Christ "for us," and God's saving action takes place independent of us, the idea of cooperation in justification is unnecessary and misleading. Once the sinner is justified, however, then the biblical images of communion, indwelling, and cooperation come into play and it is possible to speak about working out "your own salvation with fear and trembling" (Phil. 2:12).

THE SPIRITUAL LIFE

Finally, because of their different ways of conceiving of salvation, Lutherans and Orthodox understand the spiritual life differently. Lutherans generally do not speak about "penultimate" goals, of gradual growth in perfection, or of a progressive acquisition of righteousness. The Lutheran concept of *simul justus et peccator* (at the same time justified and sinner) opposes ideas of guaranteed sequential moral improvement. The Orthodox believe that "as we became not apparently but really sinful because of Adam, so through Christ, the Second Adam, we became really justified."[29] The Orthodox speak about the quest for "holiness" as a process based on divine-human cooperation. God's Holy Spirit, the "source of sanctification," bestows upon each human person the life of holiness made available in Christ, in the human nature he assumed for us. In a dynamic process, working "from within," the Holy Spirit leads human persons in the church "from strength to strength, power to power, and glory to glory." Although the Lutheran accent on grace *extra nos* (from the outside) avoids the anxieties of spiritual pulse-taking, the Orthodox find such talk of grace outside of us puzzling. If grace is only outside us and does not bring about a change in the life of the believer, justification can become a fiction that does not touch the substance of life and experience. Lutherans are uncomfortable with talk of growth in perfection and divine-human cooperation because it appears to have Pelagian overtones. In our discussions, however, it became clear that the Orthodox understand human cooperation as the work of the Holy Spirit. The initiative belongs uniquely to God who through the Spirit fills our hearts with the love of the Father. Without our active receptivity, however, God's work would come to nothing. Divine initiative must be met by a moral response on the part of the believer if the work of sanctification is to proceed.

In answer to questions from the Orthodox as to how grace can be "external," Lutherans affirm that faith is a divine work "in us" as well as "for us" and that it changes us. In Lutheran language this is the meaning of sanctification. God does not simply declare the sinner righteous; God also desires that the work of salvation be brought to fulfillment, that human beings become actually perfected. Saint Paul writes: "Not that I have already obtained this or have already reached the goal; but I press on to make it my own, because Christ Jesus has made me his own" (Phil. 3:12).

The question remains: Grace changes us in what way and to what degree? There can be no doubt that Lutherans and Orthodox view the life of faith and the quest for holiness quite differently. For the Orthodox genuine asceticism is an indispensable element in the Christian life. Asceticism has played a very small part in

Lutheran life and spirituality. Nevertheless, Lutherans and Orthodox agree that in "working out our own salvation with fear and trembling" it is God who "is at work in you [us] enabling you [us] both to will and to work for his good pleasure" (Phil. 2:13). Only through the word of the gospel, the life of prayer and worship, and participation in the sacraments can the faithful enjoy fellowship with God and be empowered to become "like him."

The Christian life is never inert and static; it is a life lived to God, a life of perpetual growth, in which we are being "changed into the same image [the Lord's] from one degree of glory to another" (2 Cor. 3:18). Christians live in hope of the day when we will see God face to face, and God will be all in all. As Saint Gregory, patriarch of Constantinople, put it in one of his "theological orations": On that day when God will be all in all, we will no longer be captive to our sinful passions, but "will be entirely like God, ready to receive into our hearts the whole God and God alone. This is the perfection to which we press on."[29]

The Communion of Saints

For both Lutheran and Orthodox, spiritual growth encompasses prayer, the study of the Scriptures, and participation in the sacramental and liturgical life of the church. We are never apart from the fullness of the communion of saints, living and dead, who join with us in praising and glorifying God the Father, Son, and Holy Spirit. In the words of the Te Deum: "The glorious company of apostles praise you. The noble fellowship of prophets praise you. The white-robed army of martyrs praise you. Throughout the world the holy Church acclaims you." Growth in the Spirit, then, is never individualistic, it always takes place in the unity of the body of Christ and is dependent on the growth of all.

Common Roots and Unity

By the power of the Holy Spirit, we have found ourselves drawn together in Christ on those topics that we had anticipated greatest disagreement. If Lutherans can begin to understand and appreciate the Orthodox emphasis on deification (*theosis*) as communion with God, and the Orthodox can begin to understand and appreciate the Lutheran emphasis on the proclamation of "justification by grace through faith," as we have done in this dialogue, then we have taken a significant step toward breaking down the wall of partition that divides us. Then we can more readily approach other differences that keep us apart, including those concerning the nature of the church.

We have shared different perspectives and emphases, both within and between our traditions, which are often complementary, mutually challenging and informative, and on which we anticipate continuing reflection, cooperation, and convergence.

In future dialogues, the Lutherans and Orthodox hope to continue in humility and respect, the exploration of our common roots within the Holy Scriptures and the early church. As we have jointly studied the Scriptures, the church fathers, and the reformers, we have learned to recognize our similarities and respect our differences, as well as to rejoice in our unity in Christ and our common confession of the one God, Father, Son, and Holy Spirit, to whom be glory now and forever.

1

Orthodox Soteriology

The doctrine of salvation (*soteria, yishoua*) holds a central place in the life of every religion, especially Christianity.

Christianity is the religion of salvation in Christ and through Christ. One of the major names of Christ is Savior (*Yeshoua, Soter*). In Saint Matthew's Gospel, the angel tells Joseph: "You are to name him Jesus, [Savior], for he will save his people from their sins" (Matt. 1:21). And Saint Paul tells the Jews in the Book of Acts: "God has brought to Israel a Savior, Jesus, as he promised" (Acts 13:23). In his speech to his compatriots the Day of Pentecost, Saint Peter told them with regard to Jesus: "There is salvation in no one else, for there is no other name under heaven given among mortals by which we must be saved" (Acts 4:12).

For the Christian in general, and the Orthodox Christian in particular, salvation can only be understood in terms of salvation in Christ. "For Christ is the head of the church, the body of which he is Savior" (Eph. 5:23).

SALVATION AS ORTHODOX CHRISTIANITY UNDERSTANDS IT

One of the texts quoted above understands salvation as "freedom from sin" (Matt. 1:21), or as "God is with us" [Emmanuel] (Matt. 1:23). According to Saint Paul, "Christ Jesus came into the world to save sinners" (1 Tim. 1:15). In the Gospels we read that "the Son of Man came to seek out and to save the lost" (Luke 19:10),

35

to heal the sick (Luke 5:31), and to call not the righteous, "but sinners to repentance" (Luke 5:32). He did not come to condemn the world, "but in order that the world might be saved through him" (John 3:17). We read that "God so loved the world that he gave his only Son, that everyone who believes in him may not perish but have eternal life" (John 3:16).

Saint Paul also tells us that through Christ, God "has rescued us from the power of darkness and transferred us into the kingdom of his beloved Son, in whom we have redemption, the forgiveness of sins" (Col. 1:13-14). Saint John the Evangelist tells us that with the coming of Christ "we have passed from death to life" (1 John 3:14). Saint Paul speculates that "if Christ has not been raised, then our proclamation has been in vain, and your faith has been in vain" (1 Cor. 15:14).

Finally, the Nicaean-Constantinopolitan Creed of the faith tells us that Christ "for us men and for our salvation came down from heaven, and was incarnate by the Holy Spirit and the Virgin Mary, and became man."[1]

To summarize the doctrine found in the texts just quoted, we would say that salvation in Christ is given to humankind through Christ's incarnation, his entire life and work, his sufferings, his death, and his resurrection from the dead. Salvation in Christ is freedom from sin, from death, and from the powers of darkness, and healing of our human nature. Ultimately, salvation is restoration of life in communion with God.

ORTHODOX CHRISTIAN SOTERIOLOGY

In the light of this summary of doctrine, I will briefly examine the following points of Orthodox Christian soteriology: presuppositions of salvation in Christ: man's fall and its consequences; salvation in Christ: the person of the Savior; salvation in Christ: the work of the Savior; salvation as sanctification: the work of the Holy Spirit; the church of Christ: the ark of salvation and the communion of saints; and fulfillment of salvation in Christ: Orthodox eschatology.

Presuppositions of Salvation in Christ: Man's Fall and Its Consequences

The Book of Genesis tells us of the creation of man: "Then God said, 'Let us make humankind in our image, according to our likeness.' . . . So God created humankind in his image, in the image of God he created them; male and female he created them"(1:26-27).

In commenting upon these texts, the Greek fathers speculate that the image of God in humans is the "great natural prerogative" of human life which makes people distinct from the rest of creation. Let me quote myself, as I summarized the doctrine in another article. According to the Greek fathers,

> man created in God's image and likeness, has a very special place in God's creation, called to be God's proxy toward His creation.
>
> Man is created as a psycho-physical unity: God "uses his hands" to create man, to show special care about man's creation. God takes dust from the earth, fashions man, and breathes into man's nostrils the "breath of life," man's soul, of a spiritual nature. Man becomes the link between the spiritual creation of God (angels) and the material one (earth), for he partakes of both. This is why "man's mission will be to bring the creation into communion with God" (Saint Maximos the Confessor).
>
> Man is created in the image of God, with the specific call to become God-like. The fathers of the Church elaborate on this doctrine of Genesis. Man's being in the image of God means that man has a spiritual soul reflecting God (the Father) as a person. Man is capable of knowing God and being in communion with God. Man belongs to God, for being God's child and image makes him God's relative. Man's soul is endowed with God's energies and life; one of these energies is love. Love, coming from God, is also directed toward God, creating union and bringing communion with God.
>
> The Fathers also make a distinction between the image of God in man, and his likeness to God: image is the potential given to man, through which he can obtain the life of *theosis* (communion with God). Likeness with God is the actualization of this potential; it is becoming more and more what one already is: becoming more and more God's image, more and more God-like. The distinction between image and likeness is, in other words, the distinction between being and becoming.
>
> Being in the image of God and called to likeness with God also means for man that God's immortality is reflected in man, insofar as man continues to be in communion with God

through God's image in him, and that man is assigned God's creation, to be God's proxy in it, to have dominion over it and keep it in touch with the Creator.

Saint Maximos the Confessor gives this noble mission to man (to Adam, the first man): man has to overcome all kinds of distinctions within God's creation, before man brings God's creation back to God: man was called to overcome the distinction between male and female, inhabited earth and paradise, heaven and earth, visible and invisible creation, and, finally, the division between created and uncreated, thus unifying God's creation with the Creator. Since man failed to achieve this union (theosis), the "New Adam," Christ, took it upon Himself to fulfill this original call of the first man (Adam).[2]

In spite of man's call to achieve *theosis*, life in communion with God, "in God's likeness," the "first Adam" failed God and failed himself. This failure, which is the essence of what in the theological language is called "sin" (missing the mark, *hamartia*, *hatta*), together with death, which is the "wages of sin" (Rom. 6:23), the general deterioration of the human nature because of its separation from the "Source of Life," God, and the submission of the fallen human nature to the "powers of darkness," Satan and his angels, is the main presupposition of the saving and deifying work of Christ.

Let me quote my own summary of the doctrine:

Man's Fall and Its Consequences

Unlike Saint Augustine's doctrine of original justice, which attributes to the first man several excessive perfections, perfect knowledge of God and God's creation, for example, that make the fall impossible, the doctrine of the Greek Fathers of the image of God in man as a potential to be actualized, allows the possibility of a deterioration, as well. Saint Irenaeus speaks of the first man (Adam) as an infant (nepios), who had to grow up to adulthood. Instead, man failed himself, by not "passing the test" of maturity given to him by God.

In spite of God's prohibition, man chose to eat from the tree of knowledge of good and evil (Genesis). Being "good by nature," man had to also become "good by choice." Unfortunately, it did not happen that way. Following the "snake's" advice (the devil's, that is), man also tried to do what the fallen angels did: to "become a god without God." Man's imperfection and innocence, or, better, naivete, and his relative pride, cultivated by the "accuser," became the cause of man's fall from

God's communion, due to his disobedience and rejection of God. Man put his purpose in himself, instead of putting it in God. Man's free will is responsible for his own decline.

The consequences of this revolt against God, which the West calls "original," and the East "ancestral" (propatorikon) sin, are that man lost his original innocence; the image of God in him was tarnished, and even became distorted; man's reason was obscured, his will weakened, the desires and passions of the flesh grew wild; man suffered separation from God, the author and source of life. He put himself in an unauthentic kind of existence, close to death. The Fathers speak of "spiritual death," which is the cause of the physical one, and which may lead to the "eschatological," eternal death: for "the wages of sin is death" (Rom. 6:23).

The state of fall, of unauthentic life close to death, this status of "spiritual death" continues to be transmitted to all of man's progeniture, even those who are born of Christian parents. The personal guilt of the first man belongs to him exclusively. However, the results of his sin are transmitted to the entire human race. A personal commitment through an engagement of one's personal free will is required, in order for things to turn around. Christ, who requires this personal commitment, made this change possible through His coming and His work upon earth.

The Case of Mary, the Mother of God

Does the Mother of God, Virgin Mary, participate in the "ancestral sin?" The question does not make much sense for the Orthodox, for it is obvious that Mary, being part of the common human race issued of the first man (Adam) automatically participates in the fallen status and in the "spiritual death" introduced by the sin of the first man.

The Fathers of the Church speculate on Luke 1:35, concluding that Mary was purified by the Holy Spirit the day of Annunciation, in order for her to become the "worthy Mother of God." However, even after she gave birth to the Son of God, Mary was not exempted of less serious ("venial") sins. Saint John Chrysostom attributes to Mary the sin of vanity, in the context of the first miracle of Christ in Cana of Galilee.

Mary was also saved by her Son, for God is her Saviour (Luke 1:47) as well. It is unfortunate that the Roman Catholic

Church promulgated the doctrine of the so-called "Immaculate Conception" in 1854, which contradicts the traditional doctrine of the Church concerning Mary.[3]

Salvation in Christ: The Person of the Savior

According to the doctrine of the church fathers, and that of the church councils, people could not have saved themselves from their sinful condition and liberate themselves from a "fallen nature"; they could not have restored the "fallen image" on their own; they could not have freed themselves from their sinful condition (separation from God's communion), and ultimately the status of death, in separation from life, which is God. People could not have freed themselves from the dynasty of the evil one, under which they subjected themselves through the fall. The only healing of this situation could have come from God.

This is why a divine person, or hypostasis, that of the Word of God had to be incarnate, to become flesh, so that he could bring humanity back to God (John 1:14). Let me again quote myself:

The Divine Plan of Salvation

Man failed God and failed himself through his revolt against God. However, God did not abandon him. God kept following man with His loving care and providence. God prepared man's salvation in the same eternal Logos of God, through whom we are created, so that even after our fall we may return to immortality (Saint Athanasius).

The plan of God for man's salvation is called the plan of "divine economy," i.e. divine dispensation. God the Father conceives the plan, the Son executes it, the Holy Spirit fulfills it and leads it to perfection and finalization.

God the Father acts out of love for man, in sending His own Son for the salvation of the world (John 3:16). When the time was ripe, after a series of purifications throughout the Old Testament that led to the Virgin Mary who could respond to God, accepting man's salvation on behalf of humankind, God sent forth His only-begotten Son, "born of woman, born under the law, to redeem those who were under the law, so that we might receive adoption to sonship" (Gal. 4:4-5).

Christ's Incarnation and the Mystery of Salvation

Christ saved humankind through what He is, and through what He did for us. Beginning with Saint Irenaeus, the Greek

Fathers continually reiterate the statement that the Incarnate Son of God "became what we are (a human being) so that we may become what He is (gods by grace)." "He became incarnate, so that we may be deified," Saint Athanasius says. By assuming our human nature, the Incarnate Logos, a divine person, brought this humanity to the heights of God. Everything that Christ did throughout His earthly life was based on the presupposition that humanity was already saved and deified, from the very moment of His conception in the womb of Mary, through the operation of the Holy Spirit.

Jesus the Christ, the God-Man

Anointed by the Holy Spirit of God since its conception, Christ's humanity is the humanity of the Messiah (the Anointed one) since the beginning of its existence.

Christ is at the same time the son of the Virgin, but also the natural Son of God, by His very nature. His humanity is a real humanity, with a body and soul, which suffered hunger and thirst, which suffered humiliation and the Cross. The Church condemned such heresies as that of the Docetists, who said that Christ's humanity was not real, Arius who taught that there was no soul in Jesus, and Apollinarius of Laodicea who taught that there was no reason in Jesus.

The Church also defended the divinity of Jesus against the Ebionites, who denied Christ's divinity, the Monarchian heresy which subordinated the Son to the Father, and Arianism, which also denied the divinity of the Logos of God. Against all these heretics the Church upheld the doctrine that Christ, a divine person, is "true God of true God," for He is the only begotten Son of God, not in a metaphorical, but a natural sense. He has the divine properties of omniscience and pre-existence in terms of God's creation. He is the only one without sin: He operates miracles through His divinity, accepts divine honor and worship due to the divinity, and accepts faith in Him.

Humanity and divinity are hypostatically united together: the two natures exist in the one person of the Word who became flesh, a divine person (or hypostasis). Christ exists "in two natures," without being of two natures; the two natures exist united together "without confusion, without change, without division, without separation" (Council of Chalcedon). The first two adverbs are addressed against the heresy of Eutyches and the monophysites who confused the natures and the last two

41

against the Nestorians, who separated and divided humanity and divinity in Christ.

Consequently, Christ has two wills also and two operations, one human and one divine; the two work together "to achieve man's salvation"; however, the human will and operation is always subjected to the divine (Third Council of Constantinople, the Sixth Ecumenical, against Monothelitism).

The consequences of this hypostatic union of the two natures in Christ are the "coinherence" of human and divine nature, the communicatio idiomatum, the natural sonship of Christ's humanity, one worship of the two natures in Christ, deification of Christ's human nature, Christ's double knowledge and power (however, attributed to one person), Christ's absolute unsinfulness, and the Mother of God being truly Theotokos and Virgin before, during, and after she gave birth to the only-begotten Son of God.[4]

The fall of humanity was a catastrophe, a "cosmic event" with catastrophic consequences for the whole cosmos; so was the incarnation of the Word of God, the "Word-becoming-flesh," which reversed the results of the fall. To quote John Meyendorff:

To affirm that God became man, and that His humanity possesses all the characteristics proper to human nature, implies that the Incarnation is a cosmic event. Man was created as the master of the cosmos and called by the creator to draw all creation to God. His failure to do so was a cosmic catastrophe, which could be repaired only by the creator Himself.

Moreover, the fact of the Incarnation implies that the bond between God and man, which has been expressed in the Biblical concept of "image and likeness," is unbreakable. The restoration of creation is a "new creation," but it does not establish a new pattern, so far as man is concerned; it reinstates man in his original divine glory among creatures and in his original responsibility for the world. It reaffirms that man is truly man when he participates in the life of God; that he is not autonomous, either in relation to God, or in relation to the world; that true human life can never be "secular." In Jesus Christ, God and man are one; in him, therefore, God becomes accessible not by superseding or eliminating the *humanum*, but by realizing and manifesting humanity in its purest and most authentic form.

The Christ-event is a cosmic event both because Christ is the Logos—and, therefore, in God the agent of creation—and because He is man, since man is a "microcosm." Man's sin plunges creation into death and decay, but man's restoration in Christ is a restoration of the cosmos to its original beauty.[5]

This restoration of creation in Christ, beginning with the restoration of the "fallen image" of God in humanity, became a reality through the person first, and then the work of the Savior, Jesus the Christ, the God-man.

In his essay on the soteriological teaching of the Greek fathers, Dr. Constantine Dratsellas says:

As far as the Soteriology of the Fathers is concerned, I should like to lay stress and underline the following points:

(1) The Fathers dealing with the Theanthropic Person of the Incarnate Logos speak also at the same time of His saving work. They never separate Jesus Christ from His redemptive work. And as Emil Brunner says: "Das Werk und Person des Erlösers sind eine unauflösliche Einheit," (Brunner E., *Der Mittler*, Zurich 1947, p. 359). They always combine the Being and the Acting of God in the Person and the work of the Redeemer. This is very important for a correct understanding of Patristic Theology and for evaluating the Patristic thought.

(2) When the Fathers speak of the Incarnation of the Logos they mean not only the Birth of Christ and His assuming human flesh but the whole Mystery of His Economy, and therefore, His Birth, His Life on earth, His Work, His Sufferings, His Death, His Resurrection. It is worth noticing that the Fathers always lay much stress on Christ's Resurrection which is the center of Christian faith and the affirmation of His Birth, His Life and His Death, etc. And when they speak of His Death, they see it in the light of His Incarnation. They see the mystery of Christ as a whole. They never separate these two aspects of this mystery. They speak of the whole Incarnate Logos and of His Saving Work, and they ascribe the Salvation of man to the whole Christ, to His whole Saving Work and not to one particular act of His life.

These conclusions lead us to a third one, so (3) the Fathers never formulated any special theories on Soteriology. They are inventions of modern theologians who form several theories and then try to find some of the Fathers as supporters of their personal ideas. This leads to a dangerous misunderstanding of Patristic theology.[6]

In the light of these statements, let us now discuss the saving work of Jesus the Savior, the incarnate Word of God who entered our human history, lived among us, taught us the truth of God, led us to salvation, suffered the cross and death for us, was resurrected on the third day for us and freed us from death and the one who has dominion over death, giving us everlasting life upon which death has no claim.

Salvation in Christ: The Work of the Savior

Christ, the incarnate Word of God, is seen in the theology of the Greek fathers as the "New Adam."[7]

As the first (old) Adam was the leader of humankind into disobedience, thus inventing sin (separation from God) and its consequence, death and deterioration of nature, so the second (new) Adam introduces obedience to God, and a life in constant communion with God for humankind. Christ, the creative Logos, created and assumed a new, perfect humanity, in constant union and communion with God, the humanity that exists only as "en-hypostasized" in the one (divine) hypostasis of the Word-who-became-flesh.

The new (second) Adam thus becomes a new model for humankind, and the one who achieves *theosis* in the human nature, through his incarnation (Saint Maximos the Confessor). Therefore, salvation, as life in communion with God, is already present in Christ's humanity on the basis of the hypostatic union of human and divine natures in Christ.

What needs to be done, is for the other obstacles to be abolished, so that humanity (and the entire cosmos in it) may be freed from the additional consequences of the "ancestral sin," that is, sin, death, and submission to the devil. My summary of the Eastern Orthodox doctrine follows:

Jesus the Prophet, the Priest, and the King

Jesus had the following obstacles to overcome in order for Him to accomplish the work for which he came (theosis): the obstacle of nature, the obstacle of sin, the obstacle of death, and the dominion of the devil. The obstacle of nature was overcome with His Incarnation; the obstacle of sin and death was overcome by the Cross and the Resurrection of Jesus. The dominion of the devil was overcome by Christ's descent into Hades (Hell).

According to Eusebius of Caesaria and the patristic tradition of the Church, the mission of Christ (continued by the Church) is threefold: Prophet, Priest, and King.

As a Prophet, Jesus taught humankind the truth of God, being Himself the Incarnate Truth, the Way and Life. Christ's teaching is characterized by clarity and lucidity, simplicity and completeness. Christ is the teacher who backs His teaching with His life.

As a Priest, Christ offers Himself as a victim "for the life of the world." Through His sacrifice on the Cross, Christ "redeems us from the curse of the law, by his precious blood," bestowing "immortality upon humankind" (Troparion of the Crucifixion). The blood shed upon the cross washes away our sin; as it fell upon Adam's (man's) skull and dry bones (according to a pious tradition Adam's tomb lay under the place of crucifixion on Golgotha) they were made alive again; man's poisonous blood was replaced with the life-giving blood of God (Troparion of the Feast of the Exaltation of the Cross). Through Christ's death upon the Cross, man was restored to life.[8]

In the Acts of the Apostles, Saint Peter accuses his compatriots of killing "the Author of Life, whom God raised from the dead" (3:15). Saint Peter also tells them: "The God of our ancestors raised up Jesus, whom you killed by hanging him on a tree. God exalted him at his right hand as Leader and Savior, that he might give repentance to Israel and forgiveness of sins" (Acts 5:30-31). In commenting upon these passages, the Greek fathers speculate that "it was not possible for death and corruption to keep the Author of Life" (Saint Basil's liturgy), and that Jesus, the new Adam, suffered death in his humanity, so that through the power of his divine hypostasis he may destroy death by enduring death and thus free humankind from death and corruption. "For suffering death upon the Cross, He destroyed death by death" (Byzantine liturgy).

The "cosmic event" of death and corruption introduced to created nature by the first Adam, is counteracted by another, the death of a divine hypostasis upon the cross. By enduring it in his humanity, by enduring separation between soul and body upon the cross, the incarnate Word of God overpowered death and the one who has dominion over death, the devil. The Greek fathers, following Saint Gregory of Nyssa, deployed the "fish-hook" interpretation of the death of Christ upon the cross. According to this interpretation, the devil and Hades dominated by it were self-deceived and defeated in trying to exercise dominion over Christ, for this was not possible. As the paschal sermon attributed to Saint John Chrysostom says: "Hades received a body, and encountered God; it received mortal dust, and met Heaven face to face."

Byzantine theology does not elaborate on the Pauline doctrine of justification through the death of Christ, as we find it in Rom. (5:16-21) and Gal. (3:13). To quote John Meyendorff, the Greek fathers

> never develop the idea in the direction of an Anselmian theory of "satisfaction." The voluntary assumption of human mortality by the Logos was an act of God's "condescension" by which He united to Himself the whole humanity; for, as Gregory of Nazianzus wrote, "what is not assumed is not healed, and what is united to God is saved": therefore, "we needed a God made flesh and put to death in order that we could live again." . . .
>
> . . . the death of Christ is truly redemptive and "life-giving" precisely because it is the death of the Son of God in the flesh . . . In the East, the Cross is envisaged not so much as the punishment of the just one, which "satisfies" a transcendent Justice requiring a retribution for man's sins. As George Florovsky rightly puts it: "the death on the Cross was effective, not as a death of an Innocent One, but as the death of the Incarnate Lord." The point was not to satisfy a legal requirement, but to vanquish the frightful cosmic reality of death, which held humanity under its usurped control and pushed it into the vicious circle of sin and corruption.[9]

The cross of Christ is an expression of not only his priestly, but also royal ministry:

> Christ is King throughout His earthly life, for He came to establish and to announce the Kingdom of God (see Matt. 4:17). However, the highlights of His Royal Ministry are the Cross itself (for, according to Saint John Chrysostom, Christ dies as the King who offers His life for His subjects); the descent into Hades to announce salvation to "those who were asleep there from all ages" (Troparion of Holy Friday); the Resurrection, through which Christ "tramples down death by death, bestowing everlasting life to the dead" (Resurrection hymn); Christ's Ascension into heaven, through which He re-enters into the Father's glory; and Christ's glorious coming again.[10]

Christ, the new Adam, not only originates a new "being" in his deified humanity; he introduces a "well-being," through his saving work, his sufferings upon the cross and the washing away of human sin through shedding upon the cross of his precious blood; upon humankind he also bestows life of immortality, "eternal being" through his glorious resurrection from the dead (Saint Maximos the Confessor).

Objectively speaking, salvation in Christ is an *efapax*, once for all given in the one event of Christ, that is his person, his life, and his work. How does this salvation in the human nature (and by extension, in all the cosmos) become a personal reality for created, human persons?

This requires the mission and involvement of another divine hypostasis, the work of the third hidden hypostasis of our triune God, who reveals Christ to us, forms Christ in us, bestows upon humankind Christ's messianic gifts, without revealing himself. He is the source of new life in Christ, the "Source of Sanctification" (Saint Basil). For every blessing comes to us from the Father through the Son, in the Holy Spirit. In a similar manner, our ascent to God happens in the light and enlightenment and the life-creating and life-giving activity of the Holy Spirit; the Spirit takes us to the incarnate Son of God; and it is in him and through him, the door and the way, that we are led to the Father, our final destination.

Salvation as Sanctification: The Work of the Holy Spirit

Salvation is not only redemption from sin and its consequences, death and the dominion of Satan; salvation is also life in communion with God, participation of abundant life in Christ, and sanctification through participation in the life of the Holy One. This sanctification is only possible through the mission and work of the Holy Spirit, the "Source of Sanctification."

Let me quote my summary:

The Mission of the Holy Spirit

The last part of the plan of salvation (divine economy) is fulfilled by the Holy Spirit of God (economy of the Holy Spirit).

The Spirit of God prepares for the coming of Christ in the Old Testament period, becomes the ointment of Christ's flesh the day of the Annunciation, accompanies Christ throughout His mission on earth, and applies Christ's work, both saving

47

and deifying, to each Christian individually, through the sacramental life of the Church. Christ has achieved our salvation and deification in an objective way, in our nature. The Spirit applies salvation and deification in a subjective way, to our persons. Divine grace, the Church and the sacraments are the workings of the Holy Spirit.

Divine Grace

By divine grace we understand the saving and deifying energy of God, made available through Christ's work, and distributed by the Holy Spirit, the source of grace and sanctification. Divine grace, the work of the Holy Spirit, is a free gift, necessary for our salvation, non-coercive, which requires our cooperation (synergy). Our response to the grace of God is our works of love, which are the fruits of God's grace working in us. We are justified by God's grace. However, this justification is not real, unless it produces the "works of righteousness."[11]

Justification and Sanctification. Saint Paul tells us that God (the Father) is the source of our lives "in Christ Jesus, who became for us wisdom, from God and righteousness and sanctification of redemption (1 Cor. 1:30). "Wisdom" refers to the person of Christ, whereas "righteousness, sanctification, and redemption" refer to his saving work. The three are taken together as synonymous; which means that redemption is righteousness (or justification) and sanctification.

Saint Paul also tells us that God predestined us "to be conformed to the image of his Son, in order that he might be the firstborn within a large family. And those whom he predestined he also called; and those whom he called he also justified; and those whom he justified he also glorified" (Rom. 8:29-30).

In this second text, Saint Paul introduces a distinction between four things: predestination, calling, justification, and glorification. However, even here these various "stages" of life in communication with God can only be seen as part of one unique process, that of sanctification. God predestines and calls all people to salvation in Christ and conformity with his glorious humanity. Then he justifies and glorifies them in a sole redemptive act, in the Holy Spirit, who is the "perfecting cause" and source of sanctification. The Spirit applies salvation in Christ to each person who is a brother or sister of the Lord Jesus.

In other words, justification is not a separate act of God but the negative aspect of salvation in Christ, which is freedom from sin, death, and the devil; whereas sanctification is the positive aspect of God's saving act, that of spiritual growth in new life in Christ communicated by God's Holy Spirit.[12]

Humanity's justification through forgiveness of sins is not a mere covering over man's sins, but a real destruction of them. It is not a mere external decision but a reality. Sins are forgiven truly and really. God does not declare someone to be justified if he [or she] is not really free. We understand this teaching better if we remember the relation between Adam and Christ.

As we became not only apparently but really sinful because of Adam, so through Christ the Second Adam we become really justified.[13]

In other words, darkness and light cannot exist together, for when light arrives, it chases away the darkness. So it is with justification in Christ; when it happens, through participation in the restored life in Christ, sinful life disappears, exactly as darkness flees the presence of light. People in communion with Christ's humanity, "conformed to the image of Christ," cannot be "sinful and righteous" at the same time, with a mere "imputed" righteousness that is a "pseudo-righteousness." Once justified, people are also sanctified by the life of Christ in the Holy Spirit.

In quoting Saint Cyril of Alexandria, Dr. Dratsellas says of sanctification:

Man's sanctification in Christ is mainly participation in the Divine Nature. When the Holy Spirit communicates Himself to a creature He makes the nature of that creature holy. To be without sin, as it is possible for man, and to be transformed to the creator's image are two inseparable ideas. This transformation and sanctification of man takes place in man not only by the grace of God, but through the Holy Spirit Himself, who "forms Christ in us" and who "renovates us to (conforms us with) God." The Holy Spirit is God and for that reason man's sanctification takes place not . . . through something like a ministerial grace, but as participation in the Divine Nature that the Spirit gives to those who are worthy.[14]

This "divine nature" in which humanity participates is not the essence of God but God's divine energies, as described previously.

Justification By Faith: Faith and Works. Objectively speaking, salvation (to be understood both as justification and sanctification) is

49

a given in Christ and the Holy Spirit. Justification in our nature is more appropriate for Christ's work; sanctification in our persons is most appropriate for the work of God's Holy Spirit. Both are the gift of God, a *gratia gratis data.*

However, in order for justification and sanctification to be real, human freedom of choice is required. God does not want to save humankind in spite of human free will and human freedom of choice.

A true "freedom of choice" according to humanity's "natural will" is the only possible choice for authentic human nature, which, as in the case of Christ, always submits itself to the divine will. However, because of what Saint Maximos calls humanity's "gnomic will," which can also choose not to submit to God's holy will, both the possibility of falling into sin and the possibility of not receiving God's free gift of salvation in Christ also exist. Ultimately, not all humankind will be saved in spite of God's desire for "everyone to be saved and to come to the knowledge of the truth" (1 Tim. 2:4).

The spirit of freedom sets humanity free, to freely choose salvation in Christ as justification and forgiveness of sins. Faith is enough, in order for this justification to come about.

Dr. Dratsellas quotes Saint Cyril of Alexandria as saying: "We are freely justified through the grace of Christ, and we have not offered anything in exchange for our lives, nor have we bought the glory of our freedom, but we gain this gift through the gentleness and philanthropia (love for man) of our Lord." Dr. Dratsellas comments: "Having been justified by grace we do not offer or rather we cannot offer anything in exchange for this great and unique gift. Man cannot offer anything to God. Man only receives from God, who always offers."[15]

Dr. Dratsellas continues: "speaking about justification on man's part Cyril teaches that true faith is the condition for the personal application of the divine gifts of Christ's sacrifice, and therefore for obtaining justification. 'It is in Christ that our access (to God) is realized, and we who are infected (by sin) come near to God, yet we are justified through faith.' " Now, this faith is true knowledge of God, not only of an intellectual, but also moral character, it is connected with repentance; it is inseparable from Christian love. It always operates through Christian love. Otherwise it cannot be true faith; otherwise, it is a "dead faith," which cannot justify man.[16]

Sanctification as Theosis.   The faith that justifies a person, as well as the love a person possesses, is the gift of God's Holy Spirit, which is inseparable from this faith. Having faith means having the Holy Spirit; having the Holy Spirit means having faith.

God's Holy Spirit, in whom sins are forgiven (justification), also begins the process of sanctification and growth in the life of sanctification. This life of sanctification is the life of Holy God, shared by the Holy One of God (Christ), and communicated by God's Holy Spirit to each created person.

The process of sanctification in God's Holy Spirit, which is participation in the life of Holy God, and includes not only human life, but the entire cosmos, is called *theosis* in the theological language of the Greek fathers. It is a transfiguration of the human nature through participation in the deifying energy of God.[17]

Acquisition of the Holy Spirit, and life of *theosis*, in communion with God, healing and transfiguration of the human nature, is the ultimate purpose of Christian life. The grounds upon which this process is possible and actually takes place is the grounds of the church of Christ.

The Church of Christ:
The Ark of Salvation and the Communion of Saints

Let me quote my summary of doctrine regarding the church:

> The place where the saving and deifying grace of the Holy Spirit is at work is the Church of Christ. The Church is at the same time the image of the Holy Trinity, the people of God, the Body of Christ, and the Temple of the Holy Spirit. All these aspects are necessary for a complete image of the Church.
>
> The Church is the great sacrament of salvation that Christ has instituted in the world. It is the Ark of Salvation, and the inaugurated Kingdom of God. Its unity is not affected by schism and heresy; its holiness is not affected by sin; its catholicity and truth is not affected by partiality and falsehood. Founded upon the Apostles, she continues the apostolic mission and ministry in the world, being the "pillar of truth," never failing in accomplishing her mission.[18]

Called by God the Father as his holy people, being in Christ and the body of Christ justified by him, sanctified by God's Holy Spirit whose temple it is, the church of Christ is founded on the life of the three divine hypostases, the life of the all blessed and Holy Trinity. As a sacred society of members, constituted as such by this communion with the three divine persons, the church is a reflection of the life of the Holy Trinity.

Mediating salvation to the world on behalf of its founder, Christ, the church sanctifies and transfigures the world, leading it to a life of *theosis* in communion with God, and leading it to God's holy kingdom, of which the church is a partial manifestation, epiphany, and inauguration.

The Ark of Salvation. The one, holy catholic and apostolic (missionary) church, which teaches the truth of Christ, leads to salvation in Christ, and sanctifies the world through the means of grace in God's Holy Spirit (sacraments), is the new ark of salvation, in which salvation in Christ is to be found.

In quoting Saint Cyril of Alexandria, Dr. Dratsellas says:

The whole Soteriology is inevitably united with the doctrine of the church because . . . her significance in the work of man's salvation is great. Cyril asserts that the church was founded not by any man but by Jesus Christ Himself, and that this church as a community of people who are united through the same correct faith in and love for Christ is not merely a natural, but a spiritual unity, which came to exist because of Christ's redemptive work and of the power of the Holy Spirit. . . . The Spiritual purpose of the church is the salvation of people, of her members.[19]

The sacraments, signs of the kingdom of God, bestow Christ's grace to its members through the operation of God's Holy Spirit. Institution and event in the life of the church do not contradict one another, but complement each other.

From the christological point of view, as the body of Christ and the grounds of organized sacramental life, the church is a sacred institution; from the pneumatological point of view, as the temple of the Spirit and the field where the Spirit of God operates, the church is a continuous Pentecost, with continuity of Pentecostal life and gifts of the Spirit, who "blows where it chooses" (John 3:8). Both aspects are inseparable from one another, and completely interdependent.

Some of the major sacraments are: the sacrament of incorporation into the life of the church, participation in Christ's death and resurrection, and beginning of the new life in Christ, the sacrament of Baptism, our personalized *pascha*; the sacrament of the gifts of the Holy Spirit, our personalized Pentecost, the sacrament of Confirmation; the sacrament of Christ's mystical presence among God's holy people, through which the deifying energies of Christ are shared with the believers who receive it, the Holy Eucharist; the sacrament of forgiveness of sins committed after baptism, which is the sacrament of Confession or Penance; the sacrament that both constitutes and unites the church as an apostolic community, guaranteeing the preaching of Christ's truth and the celebration of God's sacraments, which is the sacrament of Holy Orders (also known as Ordained Ministry or Holy Priesthood); the sacrament of perpetuation of life, Holy Matrimony; and the sacrament of Healing (Holy Oil, Oil of the Sick).

All these sacraments, means of sanctification of God's holy people, make of the church, which is a communion of human persons reflecting the Holy Trinity, a "communion of saints."

The Communion of Saints.

The Church thus conceived is not just another human organization; it is a gathering of people who profoundly share the life of faith, the new life in Christ, the life in the Holy Spirit, the life of God. The Church can best be characterized as a "communion of saints." For all its members are called to holiness, through their rite of incorporation into the Holy Body of Christ, the Temple of the Holy Spirit, the People of God. Militant on earth and triumphant in heaven, the Church is only one family sharing in the same means of grace, the holy sacraments.[20]

A communion (*koinonia*) of saints, the church is constituted as such by God's Holy Spirit, who sanctifies its life as a whole and operates through its means of sanctification: the Word and the Sacraments.

As in a continuous Pentecost, the Spirit keeps harmony and peace among the members of the church, keeping them in *koinonia* (communion) with God and with one another. The Spirit endues and endows the church with personal gifts for each member, laying stress on their variety and plurality, while keeping the unity. The Spirit endows the church with true collegiality and "synodality" at all levels, with interdependence and mutual enabling of all the church members. The Spirit directs the mission of the church toward the world, making the church the great sacrament for the world's sanctification and ultimate transfiguration through the saving work of Christ and the deifying and sanctifying operation of God's Holy Spirit.[21]

Fulfillment of Salvation in Christ: Orthodox Eschatology

In commenting on the completion of salvation in Christ at the end time according to Saint Cyril of Alexandria and the fathers of the church, Dr. Dratsellas writes:

> In Patristic Theology the doctrine of Salvation is inseparably connected with Eschatology because the state of Salvation of man is not limited to this life only. On the contrary, the work of man's Salvation will be perfect and permanent in the world of Eternity. The Second Coming is in several aspects the completion of what Christ had already initiated in the First Coming. The Judgement of the world will be completed in this Second Coming and God's time of waiting will come to an end. Man's glorious state will be in its completion in the world of eternity since the saved will be participating in the eternal glory of God.[22]

To reflect the general doctrine on salvation in Christ as being fulfilled in the eschatological times, I conclude with my summary of the Orthodox eschatological doctrine:

> The Holy Spirit of God, working through the Church and its sacramental life, leads the plan of salvation in Christ to completion and final fulfillment. The final battle with evil that operates in the world will occur just before the coming again of the Lord. In the meantime, the struggle against evil and dark forces in the world continues, with some victories on behalf of the Church, and with some failures on behalf of some of its members. This is the normal condition of the life of the Church, which is the inaugurated Kingdom of God, and which, however, has not yet come fully. Two distinct stages are to be recognized, in terms of Christian Orthodox eschatology: that of a "partial judgement," of a "partial" or "realized" eschatology, and that of a "final judgement," at the coming again of the Lord, which will come at the end of time.

Partial Judgement—The Hour of Our Death

Our physical death, a consequence of the first man's sin that we still suffer, can be seen in two ways: (1) negatively, as a kind of catastrophe, especially for those who do not believe in Christ and life everlasting in Him; and (2) positively, as the end of a maturation process, which leads us to the encounter with our Maker. Christ has destroyed the power of the "last enemy," death (1 Cor. 18:26). A Christian worthy of the name is not afraid of this physical death insofar as it is not accompanied by a spiritual or eternal (eschatological) death.

A partial judgement is instituted immediately after our physical death, which places us in an intermediate condition of partial blessedness (for the righteous), or partial suffering (for the unrighteous).

Disavowing a belief in the Western "Purgatory," our Church believes that a change is possible during this intermediate state and stage. The Church, militant and triumphant, is still one, which means that we can still influence one another with our prayers and our saintly (or ungodly) life. This is the reason why we pray for our dead. Also, almsgiving on behalf of the dead may be of some help to them, without implying, of course, that those who provide the alms are in some fashion "buying" anybody's salvation.

General Judgement—the Coming Again of Christ

The early Church lived in expectation of the "day of the Lord," the day of His coming again. The Church later realized that its time is known but to God; still, some signs of Christ's second coming were expected: (1) The Gospel will be preached everywhere in the world (Matt. 24:14; Luke 18:8; John 10:16); (2) The Jews will be converted to Christ (Rom. 11:25-26; cf. Hosea 3:5); (3) Elijah, or even Enoch, will return (Mark 9:11); (4) The Anti-Christ will appear with numerous false prophets accompanying him (1 John 2:10; 2 Thess. 2:3; Matt. 24:5); (5) Physical phenomena, upheavals, wars, suffering will occur (Matt. 24:6; Mark 13:26; Luke 21:25); and (6) The world will be destroyed by fire (ekpyrosis; see 2 Peter 3:5). All these signs are expected to be given in due time; without them, the end-time will not occur.

The resurrection of the dead is a miracle that will happen at the second coming of the Lord. According to the Creed: "I await the resurrection of the dead." This resurrection will be a new creation. However, our physical bodies as we know them now will be restored, in a spiritualized existence like that of the Lord after His Resurrection.

The final judgement will follow the resurrection of all. Some will rise to the resurrection of life, and some to the resurrection of judgement and condemnation. Christ will be our Judge on the basis of our deeds, our works of love or our acts of wickedness.

The end-time will follow, with a permanent separation between good and evil, between those who will be awarded eternal life of happiness and bliss in heaven, and those who will be condemned to the fire of eternal damnation, to the eternal remorse of their conscience for having rejected God and authentic life in Him and having joined the unauthentic life invented by the devil and his servants.

A new heaven and new earth will be established, indwelt by righteousness (2 Peter 3:13). The Kingdom of God will be fully established; the Church will cease to exist. Finally, the Son of God will turn the Kingdom over to God the Father, "that God may be everything to every one" (1 Cor. 15:28).[23]

KEYS TO UNDERSTANDING ORTHODOX SOTERIOLOGY

1. Orthodox soteriology does not limit itself to the discussion of the saving work, and especially the sacrifice on the cross of the Savior. Instead, Orthodox soteriology considers salvation as basically given in the person of the Savior, with his work only completing what is already given at the incarnation of the Word-of-God-made-flesh: *theosis*, communion between man and God, and reconciliation of man (and the world) with God.

2. With regard to understanding the "essence" of salvation in Christ, Orthodox soteriology stresses "communion in the risen body of Christ; participation in divine life; sanctification through the energy of God, which penetrates humanity and restores it to its 'natural' state, rather than justification, or remission of inherited guilt."[24]

3. With regard to understanding the sacrifice of Christ on the cross, Orthodox soteriology does not favor the Anselmian doctrine of "satisfaction." Instead, it emphasizes the "cosmic event" of the death of a divine hypostasis, the Word-of-God-who-became-flesh, so that another "cosmic event," that of human failure, sinful condition, and death may be reversed.

4. Salvation in our nature, and transfiguration in it of the whole cosmos, is achieved by the person, life, and work of Christ (Economy of the Son of God). However, this same saving and deifying work of Christ should be applied to every human person, a work that requires the mission of another divine person, God's Holy Spirit (Economy of the Holy Spirit).

5. The grace of the Holy Spirit, freely given to all, invites and incites human faith to receive salvation in Christ as justification and sanctification. In order for this faith to be real and achieve justification, it should "operate through love."

6. The church, as the "ark of salvation" and the "communion of saints," is the locus where salvation in Christ and the Spirit is to be found and accomplished. To this end the sacraments, signs of the kingdom of God—and especially the sacraments of communion (*koinonia*) with God and one another, the Holy Eucharist—are of paramount importance.

7. Finally, salvation in history finds its fulfillment in the eschatological times, when Christ will return to "judge the living and the dead," rightly rewarding or not rewarding everyone according to his or her life and acceptance or rejection of God's salvation in Christ. This final judgment will complete the whole salvation process, which begins with the incarnation of the Son of God and ends with the submission by him of God's holy kingdom to his eternal Father.

2

Humanity: "Old" and "New"— Anthropological Considerations

Today as in the past, dialogues between divided Christians are often bogged down by terminology. Thus the term *theosis* or "deification," often used to describe human destiny in Christ in Greek patristics and in Orthodox theology, provokes chills among Lutherans because of its Neoplatonic or pantheistic associations, against which they were warned by Martin Luther. In the Eastern tradition, however, the term "deification" came into use primarily to affirm a position that Lutherans generally cherish: salvation and "new" life originates in God himself, not in any inferior or created intermediary. It is against Arians that Saint Athanasius coined his famous sentence: "God assumed humanity so that we might become God."[1] It is against Nestorians that Saint Cyril of Alexandria fought for the idea that God alone saves, so that Christ the Savior was one person, that of the Son of God, making it inevitable to say that his humanity was God's humanity. It is in virtue of these christological positions that the term "deification" became legitimized in spiritual and ascetical literature, serving also, inevitably, as a bridge between Christians and Neoplatonists—a bridge that brought Greek intellectuals to the Christian faith.

In no way renouncing the legitimacy of the word *theosis* when it is used in a proper christological context, I would like to emphasize its implication for understanding another term—a fully biblical one—and one acceptable for both Lutherans and Orthodox when they speak about salvation. This term is "sanctification." Can one be sanctified other than through participation in God, who "alone is holy"?

The issue at stake is not the word "deification" but the understanding of salvation as "participation" in God's being, as the restored content and goal of human existence. The importance of that issue is stressed clearly and systematically in a recent dissertation by a Finnish Lutheran theologian who used a Greek term for "participation" (*methexis*) as the title of a book on contemporary Orthodox theology.[2] He could have chosen other terms such as *metokhe, koinonia,* or their derivatives. These terms are used in the New Testament to designate the relations between God and humanity either before the incarnation, when those relations are seen as broken or defective, or after Christ's resurrection as they were restored by grace.

THE "OLD ADAM"

The best way to understand this particular crucial dimension of anthropology as it is perceived in the Orthodox tradition is to recall the theology of Saint Irenaeus of Lyons. The advantages of starting with Saint Irenaeus is that he is still very close to the New Testament; his thought and his terminology are less suspect of being influenced by Greek philosophical categories than that of the later fathers. Actually, Saint Irenaeus anticipated Athanasius and launches the sentence: "The Word became what we are so that we might become what He is" (*Adv. haereses* V, *praef.*). His anthropological thought presupposes a certain "divinity" of the human being in the act of creation. In describing the "image of God," he presents his well-known scheme: "There are three elements of which the complete man is made up, flesh, soul and Spirit; one of these preserves and fashions the man, and this is the Spirit; another is given unity and form by the first, and this is the flesh. The third, the soul, is midway between the first two . . ." (*Adv. haer.* V,9,1). The paradox in such passages as these is that for Saint Irenaeus the "Spirit" (a term I intentionally capitalize) is identical with the Spirit of God. "The complete man," he writes, "is a mixture and union, coexisting of a soul which takes itself the Spirit of the Father, to which is united the flesh which was fashioned in the image of God . . ." (*Adv. haer.* V,6,1).

The fall consisted of the human rejection of the Spirit which was a part of humanity itself. This was a rejection of God's image and therefore of freedom, reducing human life to an "animal" condition determined by fleshly needs and to inevitable mortality.

Thus, fallen humanity is no longer "complete" humanity because it has lost participation in divine life.

For a theology accepting as necessary premise the "autonomy" of creatures and the clear distinction if not opposition between "nature" and "grace," such passages can be read only as imperfect expressions of a still inadequate and undeveloped theological thinking. But the fact is that in the East, Saint Irenaeus's conception was never thought of as detrimental to the Creator's transcendence, but, on the contrary, as an expression of God's almighty power in creating human beings, bearing his image and oriented toward him in such a way that they cease to be really human when the organic participation and relationship through the Spirit is broken.

Furthermore, Saint Irenaeus presents the relationship as a dynamic one. He does not imply that, following the fall, the Spirit simply and totally disappears from human existence; that human life is depraved completely to the point of becoming animal. Against the Gnostics, Saint Irenaeus defends the providential activity of God in the Old Testament and is the first among Christian writers to point to the role of Mary as the new Eve, able—on behalf of fallen humanity—to exercise her freedom in answering God's call: "Eve by her disobedience brought death upon herself and all the human race: Mary, by her obedience, brought salvation" (*Adv. haer.* III,22,4). This function of Mary, as the new Eve, is recognized by two other Christian writers of the second century, Justin and Tertullian. It represents a consensus in early Christian soteriology; a consensus affirming that in Mary's person, humanity, after the fall, remained capable of free choice and of joining in with God's saving act.

Aside from the veneration of Mary, which will be further developed following the definition of her "divine motherhood" at Ephesus (A.D. 431), the Eastern Christian tradition, preserved in the Orthodox church today, also venerates the just ones of the Old Testament. The "ancestors" of Christ, "Saint" Elijah, each prophet individually, and even the Maccabees brothers figure prominently in the Eastern church calendar, although they lived before grace came and were not baptized. . . . The absence of Old Testament "saints" in the Western calendar must be the result of the overwhelming impact of Augustinism, which, on this point, ignored the implications of such passages as John 8:56 ("Your ancestor Abraham rejoiced that he would see my day; he saw it and was glad").

The "justice" of the Old Testament saints was fulfilled in Christ. In him there occurred a "consummation," or "recapitulation," literally "re-heading" (*anakephalaiosis*, cf. Eph. 1:10) of humanity. The Spirit whose guiding role had been denied and rejected became the spirit of man again. Christ "consummated all things in himself by joining man to Spirit and placing Spirit in man. He himself became the source of the Spirit, and he gives Spirit to be the source of man's life" (*Adv. haer.* III,21,1).

This approach implies that in Christ there was a restoration of the true human nature, not an external addition of "grace" to an otherwise autonomous human existence. Salvation does not consist in an extrinsic "justification"—although this "legal" dimension is fully legitimate whenever one approaches salvation within the Old Testament category of the fulfillment of the law (as Paul does in Romans and Galatians)—but in a renewed communion with God, making human life fully human again.

What then is "new humanity" manifested again in Christ? Since the time of Origen, Christian thought has known the temptation of conceiving it in a Platonic sense as the restoration of some eternal state from which the fall was an accidental deviation. It is this philosophical temptation that led Origen to his theory of "preexisting souls" and eternal creation, which obscured the biblical vision of God as Creator and Master of time itself.[3] This temptation has reappeared in the so-called "sophiological" school of modern Russian religious philosophy. Writing about the incarnation as a historical event, Sergius Bulgakov asks plainly: "Do people sufficiently realize that this dogma [of the Incarnation] in itself is not primary, but derivative? In itself it demands the prior existence of absolutely necessary dogmatic formulations concerning a *primordial God-man-hood*" (italics mine).[4] Such a view, akin to some approaches of philosophical theology in the West (e.g., Paul Tillich) is hardly consistent with the patristic concept of human nature, although the fathers have been disciples of Origen. Their reinterpretation of Origenism consisted precisely in affirming creation *ex nihilo* and in time, and thus maintaining a vision of God as the absolutely transcendent and different one, so that "God-talk" could not be determined by logical necessities, or philosophical formulations.

Communion between God and the human being created by him is a "free" gift of God and requires a "free" response. It reflects divine will or "energy" and human *metanoia*—or free "change of mind," away from sin and death. This communion implies that God remains totally transcendent in his essence but communicates himself, as he wills, by grace. On humanity's side there is necessarily a movement, a process, an ascent toward God, an ascent that Saint Gregory of Nyssa defines in terms of an eternal "tension" (*epektasis*), because God is inexhaustible. The tension, however, is not one of frustration, but one of constantly realized hope, an act of life, being fulfilled over and over again.

This concept of divine communion, which is the content of that which is "new" in Christ, is based on christological and pneumatological realities. The incarnation was an assumption by the Second Person of the Trinity of a humanity which was "fallen"— in need of restoration and salvation. The Son of God became like us in every way "yet without sin" (Heb. 4:15). The New Testament tells us that he experienced human development and temptations, and only the power of his divine personhood prevented him from succumbing to them (cf. Matt. 4:3, 7). It is as he remained human, through his human will—obedient to the end, to death on the cross, that the power and glory of God was fully manifested in his resurrection. But humanity is necessarily temporal, and even in Jesus, the incarnated Son of God, the transition from the "old" to the "new" required human effort and development (it did not occur by instant, magic fiat at the second of the incarnation). Christ's humanity was therefore a "paschal" humanity; as God, he won a human battle, which humans alone could not win. The Son of God fought it humanly, "like us . . . ," and won.[5]

The pneumatological aspect of anthropology is the key to understanding human freedom. In the terminology of Saint Irenaeus, fallen humanity is a humanity deprived of the Spirit. Human life is then determined by the flesh, it is a determinism that inevitably leads to morality. Authentic freedom, truth, and life belong to God and are communicated to people by the Spirit. Each human person as well as the human community once endowed with the presence of the Spirit, ceases to be carnal, is adopted by the Father, and thus is being freed from servitude; acquiring the power, dignity, and freedom of divine sonship.

ETHICS OF THE RESURRECTION

If we accept the view that "nature" and "grace" are not opposed to each other and that "natural" human life presupposes communion with God, are not we actually reducing the Christian message to eschatology? If salvation is a "process" and if Jesus "grew in wisdom," and then went through a human death, until his new spiritual, "deified" humanity was made manifest to those who became witnesses of his post-resurrection appearances, how are we to define Christian ethics within this world? What are the basic imperatives of Christian behavior and conduct, and are they connected with the affirmations of a "theological anthropology"?

It seems to me that the answer to these questions lies entirely in the "good news," and in the power of life, anticipating the ultimate fulfillment already at work in creation and accessible to humans in Baptism. The alternative between life and death dominates the writings of the New Testament. Baptism—in its original meaning, in its traditional liturgical forms, in its significance as the ultimate commitment to Christ—implies a "new birth," the beginning of life in the kingdom. This dimension of Baptism does not exclude the idea that we are baptized "for the remission of sins," but (as noted in this volume by John Breck) Orthodox tradition does not hold the notion of an "inherited guilt," coming from Adam, but rather recognizes an inherited mortality ("sins" being free acts are remitted in the case of adult baptisms). Thus the gift of new life stands as the central meaning of the baptismal mystery. This gift is the foundation of Christian living and defines Christian behavior because it liberates believers from the determinism of mortality—from the dependence upon death.

Baptized Christians are no longer "held in slavery by the fear of death" (cf. Heb. 2:15). Death does not reign as it "exercised dominion from Adam to Moses, even over those whose sins were not like the transgression of Adam" (Rom. 5:14). This is the reason why as Christians we can stop worrying about "what we will eat or what we will drink," and can become like "birds of the air" (Matt. 6:25-26). Such utterings in the Sermon on the Mount would be mere sentimentalism, if they did not reflect the new Christian freedom from the determinism of this world, where humanity is alive "by bread alone." If Baptism is really the beginning of a new life in the kingdom, there is no reason for the baptized to struggle for survival. In patristic commentaries on Romans 5, one finds a remarkably realistic analysis of the consequences of inherited mortality, as the real reason and foundation of sinfulness. "Having become mortal," writes Theodoret of Cyrus, "[Adam and Eve] conceived mortal children, and mortal beings are necessarily subject to passions and fears, to pleasures and sorrows, to anger and hatred" (*In Rom, Patrologia graeca* 80, col. 1245A). In fact, mortality and death make struggle for survival inevitable, and create conditions for a Darwinian world, where the fittest survive, but only at the expense of the weakest. Death is the enemy from which one seeks security, and in the fallen world there is no other security than the means of the world: money, power, competition, often violence—the ingredients of sinfulness. All these are unavoidable until death is vanquished, together with all the impulses for a worldly struggle for survival.

In the world, the struggle is actually hopeless, because death can only be postponed, not ultimately suppressed. The ultimate victory is that of Christ, a victory that is the Christian "good news" and the foundation of our hope. The "life in Christ" that begins at Baptism is a life free from death. The Christian martyrs were venerated from the beginnings of Christianity; by their deaths they witnessed to this new life, just as the apostles, who had seen the risen Jesus with their own eyes. Christians, therefore, need not struggle for survival. Since they have life in themselves, they have the power to give, to serve, to live for others, without being concerned for their own survival interests.

Christian ethics is not a voluntary obligation, it is the manifestation of true life, an ethics of the resurrection.

Bibliography

Lossky, Vladimir, *On the Image and Likeness*. Crestwood, NY: Saint Vladimir's Seminary Press, 1974.

Burghardt, W. J., *The Image of God in Man According to Cyril of Alexandria*. Washington, DC: Catholic University Press, 1957.

Schmemann, Alexander, *For the Life of the World*. Crestwood, NY: Saint Vladimir's Seminary Press, 1973.

Meyendorff, John, *Byzantine Theology. Historical Trends and Doctrinal Themes*. New York: Fordham University Press, 1987.

Meyendorff, John, "New Life in Christ: Salvation in Orthodox Theology." *Theological Studies* 50 (1989), 481–99.

3

Salvation as Justification and *Theosis*

And the angel said to them, "Be not afraid; for behold, I bring you good news of a great joy which will come to all the people: for to you is born this day in the city of David a Savior, who is Christ the Lord."   Luke 2:10-11 [RSV]

Salvation is what Christianity is all about, the reason it is gospel: "good news of great joy." It was for this—to bring salvation to the world—that the Word of God became flesh and was born in the city of David; for this that the true Lord of this world suffered on a cross and conquered death by his love; for this that the holy ministry was ordained, that through the sacraments and preaching the Holy Spirit might create saving faith. It is to receive this wondrous gift that Christians come to the manger of the divine liturgy; and it is in thanksgiving for this gift that they live to the praise of his glory. As theologian Carl Braaten has written: "The whole of theology is inherently developed from a soteriological point of view. Salvation is not one of the main topics, along with the doctrine of God, Christ, church, sacraments, eschatology, and the like. It is rather the perspective from which all these subjects are interpreted."[1]

    This soteriological point of view that has shaped theology and ethics is God's revelation in Christ, committed to the apostles and their successors, made tangible and personal in the sacraments, recorded in the Holy Scriptures, and given creedal articulation by the early ecumenical councils. The great value of the Nicene Creed (with its confession of faith in Jesus Christ as "of one being with the Father," who came down from heaven "for us and for our salvation") is not merely that it is "one of the few threads by which the tattered fragments of the divided robe of Christendom are held together"[2] but that it tells us who God is and that we are saved.

Both Lutheran and Orthodox Christians, whatever their differences, have developed all of theology from this soteriological perspective. For the Orthodox, according to Metropolitan Emilianos:

> The Nicene Creed is generally accepted as providing a summary of our Christian faith. It has been used by all, from the time of its origin, as the basis of the faith of the baptized; it is proclaimed by all of us during eucharistic assemblies. . . . [It] passes from the creation to Christ's incarnation in order to show the depth and the immense love of God for human beings. He was incarnate for us, for our salvation. . . . This condescendence of Christ is linked to the institution of the church which exists in order to continue Christ's redeeming action, to bring human beings to the blessings of the Holy Trinity, and to create a *koinonia*. Here lies the mystery of the church's mission on earth. Thus Christology is linked with ecclesiology and soteriology.[3]

For Lutherans, confession of the creeds of the ancient church is one of the ways to identify themselves as standing in continuity with the one, holy, catholic, and apostolic church.[4] The placement of the creeds at the beginning of the Lutheran *Book of Concord*,[5] and frequent references to them throughout that book, demonstrate that the Lutheran confessional documents are in accord with the faith of the whole church. Historian Eric W. Gritsch (in an article on "The Origins of the Lutheran Teaching on Justification") points out that the Augsburg Confession—the primary document in the *Book of Concord*—begins with a restatement of "the trinitarian dogma in accordance with the Nicene Creed, with a heavy emphasis on its soteriological function."[6]

However, in spite of their common rootage in the soteriological perspective and confessions of the early church, the theological developments of Orthodoxy and Lutheranism—in virtual isolation from one another—have resulted in significant differences, not least in the way they speak of salvation.

It was of course the issue of salvation that prompted Luther to challenge the teaching and practice of the medieval church in the West. "The Reformation was . . . a theological debate, occasioned by a deeply existential question, anxiety over sin, and therefore fundamentally a question of soteriology."[7] While the Christian church has never produced a dogma concerning its basic soteriological proclamation, Lutherans are convinced that "the nearest thing to it is the doctrine of justification by grace alone, received through faith alone—the chief article of the Lutheran confessional writings."[8] Similarly, Gritsch and Jenson assert: "The single great proposed dogma of the Reformation was 'justification by faith alone, without the works of the law.' It is well-known that the Lutheran reformers proclaimed this as the doctrine by which the church 'stands or falls' " (*articulis stantis et cadentis ecclesiae*).[9]

Luther found this understanding of salvation expressed in the Christology of the ancient church.

> In Luther, Christology and soteriology are intimately connected with each other, as they are in Athanasius, or Cyril of Alexandria, except that Luther makes the connection much more explicit. Christology is realized in the doctrine of justification, and the doctrine of justification is nothing else but a summary of Christology in soteriological perspective.[10]

Orthodoxy had long since followed a different course. Timothy Ware describes the beginning of this course, in which another aspect of Christology was emphasized:

> Man, so the New Testament teaches, is separated from God by sin, and cannot through his own efforts break down the wall of separation which his sinfulness has created. God has therefore taken the initiative: He became man, was crucified, and rose from the dead, thereby delivering him from the bondage of sin and death. This is the central message of the Christian faith. . . .
>
> Saint Paul expressed this message of redemption in terms of *sharing:* Christ shared our poverty that we might share the riches of His divinity. "Our Lord Jesus Christ, though he was rich, yet for your sake became poor, that you through his poverty might become rich" (2 Cor. 8:9). In Saint John's Gospel the same idea is found in a slightly different form. Christ states that He has given His disciples a share in the divine glory, and He prays that they may achieve union with God: "The Glory which thou hast given me I have given to them, that they may be one even as we are one, I in them and thou in me, that they may become perfectly one" (John 17:22-23).

The Greek Fathers took these and similar texts in their literal sense, and dared to speak of man's deification (in Greek, *theosis*). If man is to share in God's glory, they argued, if he is to be "perfectly one" with God, this means in effect that man must be "deified": he is called to become by grace what God is by nature. Accordingly Saint Athanasius summed up the purpose of the Incarnation by saying: "God became man that we might be made god" [*On the Incarnation of the Logos*, 54].[11]

Is there a basic difference between this central theological concept of Orthodoxy and the doctrine that Lutherans describe as "the article on which the church stands or falls"—or is there perhaps a fruitful complementarity? This question stands before us as we examine the Lutheran point of view on salvation in light of the Orthodox emphasis on *theosis*.

THE WORD OF GOD

God's Word and faith are above everything, above all gifts and personal worth.   Martin Luther[12]

In view of the vast extent and variety of Luther's literary accomplishments and his lack of systematization, the determination of his position on a given topic is no easy task.[13] But to find the controlling perspective of his theology is not difficult—and much more important; for from the perspective with which Luther began, one may speak with some confidence even on matters which he himself did not discuss.

Luther's interpreters have employed a profusion of terms and phrases to express this perspective. However, that simply illustrates the difficulty of stretching mortal language to state the essentially inexpressible wonder that, by his own initiative, God addresses us. "The Word of God" is the biblical term for this divine self-expression, ultimately and finally revealed in Jesus Christ. For Luther, the premise and key to all theology is the fact that God has addressed us—and this self-disclosure is love.

In a sermon on John 3:16 he wrote:

During my twenty years in the cloister I was obsessed with the one thought of observing the rules of my order. We were so drowned in the stupor of our own good works that we did not see and understand these words ["God so loved the world that he gave his only Son, that whoever believes in him should not perish but have eternal life."]. But if you want to find God, then inscribe these words in your heart.[14]

"For God is a glowing furnace of love, reaching even from the earth to the heavens,"[15] a *quellende Liebe*[16] that flows with wonderful prodigality from the heart of God, to which "all creatures bear witness"[17]—"except man and the devil."[18]

Although Luther uses the term "Word of God" in several senses (thereby referring alternatively to the Bible, law, gospel, preaching, and the sacraments, as well as Christ—to whom they all bear witness), its central thrust for him was always that "God, to whom he could not rise, had come to him; that the righteousness of God which he could not satisfy had been bestowed; . . . and that in Jesus Christ that gift was proffered out of the initiative, the measureless and the shocking love of God."[19]

Since the means which God employs make him available to the humblest person, it was not only foolish but blasphemous in Luther's opinion to look anywhere for God except where God himself draws near and condescends in love to speak.[20]

Although he is present in all creatures, and I might find him in stone, in fire, in water, or even in a rope, for he certainly is there, yet he does not wish that I seek him there apart from the Word, and cast myself into the fire or the water, or hang myself on the rope. He is present everywhere, but he does not wish that you grope for him everywhere. Grope rather where the Word is, and there you will lay hold of him in the right way. Otherwise you are tempting God and committing idolatry.[21]

From his understanding of Christology, Luther was certain that no intellectual exertions or privileged, gnostic insights were called for. God uses special places, particular symbols, and specific experiences; "when God reveals Himself in some sign, no matter what its nature, one must take hold of Him in it."[22] "Nobody will obtain salvation through so-called spiritual speculations, without external things. Attention must be paid to the Scripture, and Baptism must be sought. The Eucharist must be received, and absolution must be required. . . . The Holy Spirit works nothing without them."[23]

God is infinitely greater than these signs, but he speaks through a "mask" or "veil" in order to reach us where we with our limitations and imperfections can comprehend him: the Word made flesh in Jesus Christ "for us and for our salvation," attested by the Bible, the sacraments, and the witness of the saints. "The incarnate Son of God . . . is the covering in which the Divine Majesty presents Himself to us with all His gifts, and He does so in such a manner that there is no sinner too wretched to be able to approach Him."[24]

However, even Jesus—"the only historical concretion of which we dare say unconditionally, '*Here* is the Word of God' "[25]—was not recognized as God's Word by those who crucified him, for such knowledge constitutes the gift of faith that comes only by the grace of God. "No one can correctly understand God or His Word unless he has received such understanding immediately from the Holy Spirit."[26] In nature and even in the mighty acts of God in history we are confronted by the veiled *Deus Absconditus*, and no amount of "objective investigation" can penetrate the veil or hear the Word of the *Deus Revelatus*—"for by grace you have been saved through faith, and this is not your own doing; it is the gift of God" (Eph. 2:8).

> That person does not deserve to be called a theologian who looks upon the invisible things of God as though they were clearly perceptible in those things [which have been made] (Romans 1:20). He deserves to be called a theologian, however, who comprehends the visible and manifest things of God seen through suffering and the cross.[27]

Luther scorned all attempts of unaided human reason to obtain a natural knowledge of God as a futile "theology of glory"—an approach that magnifies personal achievements instead of the incarnation of God in Jesus. Such an approach to theology rests on the speculation that human efforts are instrumental in obtaining God's forgiveness of sins and salvation. In medieval scholastic theology, salvation was described as a process to which people contribute by combining their serious intentions and righteous deeds with the sacraments—a combination of grace and the best actions of men and women.

In the "theology of the cross," however, the contemplation of "Jesus Christ and him crucified" (1 Cor. 2:2) awakens faith to hear the gospel that God justifies sinners by grace alone through faith alone for the sake of Christ alone, apart from works of the law.

Law and Gospel

What can be understood by a "theology of glory" and all human reason in general is God's will for human life, which appears both in the Mosaic Law and in natural law (*lex naturalis*). To Luther, the sum of all Christian doctrine is contained in a proper distinction between law and gospel. God deals with the world through both law and gospel, the law revealing sin and the gospel disclosing salvation. Since it is impossible for sinful human beings to achieve the perfect love demanded by God's law, the result is that sin and despair are intensified simply by the awareness of God's total claim on life. According to the Apology to the Augsburg Confession, *lex semper accusat* (the law always accuses).[28]

> With these words [Melanchthon] expresses in the most concise formula not only Luther's view, but also Paul's. . . . Consequently, the law can never be only a rule for life. It has always exercised this accusatory function, according to the testimony of the entire Holy Scriptures both before Christ and after Christ, and it will do so also in the final judgment. It functions this way for every single individual, for the godless as well as for the so-called righteous, and also for the regenerate.[29]

God's law exposes sin but cannot cure it, and therefore its greatest benefit for mankind is to convince people of their radical sinfulness so that, despairing of ever overcoming such sin, they may understand the significance of God's merciful grace in Jesus Christ. Although Luther also pointed to another benefit of the law (its importance in maintaining order in the world—the *usus legis politicus*), he saw that the principal teaching of Scripture concerning the law was this accusatory *usus legis paedagogicus* whereby people are driven to Christ.

It is important to note that the Formula of Concord also sanctions a third *usus legis didacticus*, in opposition to those who would adopt an antinomian view—a use of the law that not only rebukes sins but gives instruction about good works, thus enabling us to "learn from the law to live and walk in the law."[30] However, one must beware that, in such a use, one is not led to take the law as a way of salvation and seek righteousness by works.

> The law tells us what we ought to do; the gospel declares what God does. The law demands and threatens; the gospel gives and forgives. . . .
> But even after the reception of forgiveness, the law enters as a threat. It tries to legalize the gospel. This happens when preachers announce: "You are saved by grace, but . . . ." Grace is not grace if there are any ifs, ands, and buts about it. Grace

is unconditional. There is no salvation based on works. The sinner is incapable of doing God-pleasing works. For the Christian it is nothing less than a blasphemy to tie salvation to one's own good works, for that detracts from the sufficiency of Christ. . . .

All is of grace that nothing shall be of works, not even the work of believing the true doctrines of the faith. The ladders of free will, reason, and religious emotion are all stripped away so that faith may stick to the ground of God's grace in the earthly Christ.[31]

Grace and Righteousness

In Jesus Christ—the Word made flesh, "full of grace and truth"— God's inmost nature of love addresses humanity as the forgiveness of sins and the offer of salvation; in him what was perceived as almighty power and law throughout nature is now seen to be grace. The divine nature that is expressed in the Word and the initiative that God takes in turning toward humanity "while we still were sinners" (Rom. 5:8) are characteristics enclosed within the term "grace." Without God's grace there could be no salvation, for the encounter in which God becomes known, his message is comprehended, and the energies of his grace are realized is beyond human power to effect. God must take the initiative, for with regard to salvation the human will is in bondage to sin.

In recovering the centrality of God's grace,[32] Luther emphasized its redemptive function in Christ for human salvation. Although his vision was by no means confined to this focus, grace had to be clarified as the "divine favor" given freely out of love rather than a goodness-producing substance available only through ecclesiastically defined obedience.[33]

Beyond the historical circumstances that gave rise to and shaped this emphasis, stands the cosmic vision of Luther's christological insights developed in controversies with Zwingii; and from these insights it is clear that Luther perceived God's grace as the ground and source of all existence, the manifold expression of his self-giving, the reason why there is something rather than nothing, the fountainhead of a world marked eternally as his own.[34] Yet more than that, grace represents the involvement of God in the processes of the world: not only is he good in himself but he is loving—so loving that he sends forth his Word not simply to fabricate the infinite variety of creation but to save it from evil and bring it to fulfillment.

The revolutionary doctrine of justification by grace alone through faith alone for the sake of Christ alone is precisely what makes the "good news" good. That it had been beyond the comprehension of many Christians in every generation (and would remain so) was no surprise to Luther. In the very beginning of the Bible, works-righteousness makes its appearance in the voice of the serpent, who urges Eve to seize heaven for herself—to go ahead and eat of the fruit: "you will be like God." Luther knew from personal experience that nothing is more seductive than the appeal of self-justification.

But Luther also knew, from his personal quest for a gracious God and from his study of the Scriptures and the fathers, that it is not by striving that one comes to fulfillment and enters the kingdom of heaven. His expression of the soteriological implications of the Nicene dogma was much more intimately connected to the dogmatic development of the early church than to late medieval Catholicism. One has come down from heaven "for us and for our salvation," and God's undeserved and undeservable grace has given forgiveness, life, and salvation.

Affirming that we are *simul justus et peccator,* Luther stated that the Second Article of the Nicene Creed means that God "has completely given himself to us, withholding nothing."[35] Jesus Christ "is my Lord, who has redeemed me . . . not with silver and gold but with his holy and precious blood and with his innocent sufferings and death, in order that I may be his. . . ."[36] "How can these two contradictory things both be true at the same time, that I am a sinner and deserve divine wrath and hate, and that the Father loves me?"[37] Since the paradox is between being righteous and being a sinner, "there is therefore now no condemnation for those who are in Christ Jesus" (Rom. 8:1).

In the midst of his struggle to win God's favor Luther discovered that God's righteousness was not—as contemporary theology then taught—the terrible judgment of God upon human sins but God's free bestowal of righteousness.[38] One's best works "are mortal sins if they are judged according to God's judgment and severity and not accepted as good by grace alone."[39] The only righteousness "consists not in our works—however harmless or holy they might be—but in the forgiveness of sins and in the grace of God."[40]

Because God looks upon Christ instead of the sinner and awards Christ's righteousness to the sinner, the whole person is righteous and holy, i.e., "hidden in Christ." "The whole person, in respect both of person and of works, shall be accounted and shall be righteous and holy through the pure grace and mercy which have been poured out upon us so abundantly in Christ."[41] If Christ's righteousness is given to the sinner, he is entirely righteous, not partially so.

The Reformation doctrine of imputed righteousness safeguards the unconditional character of God's promises in Christ. Correctly understood, "righteousness" is the focus for comprehending the Word: applied to God, "righteousness" means his merciful "grace"; applied to mankind it means "justification"—the free gift that simply accounts people acceptable without regard for their sins.[42] Commenting on Gal. 2:21 ("If justification comes through the law, then Christ died for nothing"), Luther wrote: "In ordinary conversation, 'righteousness' is that virtue by which everyone gets what is coming to him. In [the New Testament], righteousness is faith in Jesus Christ."[43]

FAITH

The article on justification is a master and prince over all kinds of doctrine and rules the church and all conscience. Without it the world is dreary and nothing but darkness.

Martin Luther[44]

The doctrine of justification by faith with its christological focus and Trinitarian presuppositions was described by Luther in the Smalcald Articles in 1537 as the "first and chief article."

The first and chief article is this, that Jesus Christ, our God and Lord, "was put to death for our trespasses and raised again for our justification" (Rom. 4:25). . . .

Inasmuch as this must be believed and cannot be obtained or apprehended by any work, law, or merit, it is clear and certain that such faith alone justifies us, as Saint Paul says in Romans 3, "For we hold that a man is justified by faith apart from works of law" (Rom. 3:28), and again, "that he [God] himself is righteous and that he justifies him who has faith in Jesus" (Rom. 3:26).

Nothing in this article can be given up or compromised, nor can any believer concede or permit anything contrary to it, even if heaven and earth and things temporal should be destroyed.[45]

In his most famous treatise, Luther declared that justification occurs in the "joyous exchange" of Christ's righteousness and human sin.[46]

God is the one who acts in justifying sinners, for as Christ said, "apart from me you can do nothing" (John 15:5). Faith receives the righteousness of God, the *iustitia aliena* of Christ, and it is this act performed outside of us (*extra nos*) by which faith is accounted as righteousness. Since sin is not merely the failure to do good or the despair over such failure, but is, above all, the temptation to trust in one's own righteousness, we must have this perfect "alien" righteousness for our salvation—for that righteousness exposes sin as both presumption and despair and attacks it in its totality.

"We should not lean to our own strength, . . . but to that which is external to ourselves, namely, the promise and truth of God which cannot lie";[47] and this Word of promise and truth that comes from beyond ourselves breaks through to us only when we have acknowledged and received the gift of faith. Neither God's commands nor his promises are intelligible without faith. That God was truly in Christ is a vision shared only by those in whom the Word has created its reality; and only the heart enlivened by faith can receive the Word or deal with it. Faith is the central, controlling factor for humanity.

But just what is faith? Clearly it is not reducible to catechetical formulae or the intellectual acceptance of doctrines. Faith is the matrix, mode, or stance in which life is centered, making a person what he or she is; and Christian faith is the relationship in which God is the all-determining factor.

Faith is a miracle of grace, not a human possibility. . . . To be sure, faith is a good work, but it is the good work of the Spirit. Faith alone means Christ alone, for faith is the awareness worked by the Spirit that salvation is not from us, but for us. Faith is not the response of a person's free will to choose the grace of God. The [Lutheran] Confessions slam the door on free will to keep out every possible synergistic intrusion. They reject the statement used by some of the ancient Fathers that God draws, but draws the person who is willing. Instead, God makes unwilling persons willing to do the will of Christ.[48]

Nothing but faith in Christ alone—belonging to Christ alone—makes sinners pleasing to God. Whatever is to stand before the throne of God must be perfect. Nothing perfect is to be found except the perfect work of Christ, which work is reckoned as their own to those who cling to Christ in faith. "Since all have sinned and fall short of the glory of God, they are now justified by his grace as a gift through the redemption that is in Christ Jesus, whom

God put forward as a sacrifice of atonement by his blood, effective through faith" (Rom. 3:23-25).

Such good as is in the world does not represent the improvement of Christians, for nothing can be any more improved than the sinner who has Christ's righteousness thrown over him or her. Nothing need be or can be added to faith. "Faith makes the person, the person does good works; good works make neither the faith nor the person."[49] To confuse works with faith, law with gospel, or sanctification with justification is to make all the promises of God concerning the forgiveness of sin and everlasting life unintelligible and uncertain. The divine promise is clear and certain, so that faith may firmly depend upon it (cf. Rom. 4:16).

It was precisely this gospel which, in letters written to Melanchthon at Augsburg, Luther urged not be compromised; for this is the "article by which the Church stands or falls": "that we live by faith and by faith alone."[50]

Word and faith (the so-called "formal" and "material" principles of the Reformation) thus issue in the call to participate in creative love: the universal spiritual priesthood of all the baptized (the "ethical" principle of the Reformation). Set free by grace from concern over his or her stock of "virtue," the Christian may give unreserved attention to his or her calling in the world—"a perfectly free sovereign of all, subject to none" and yet "a perfectly dutiful servant of all, subject to all."[51]

THE PRIESTHOOD OF ALL THE BAPTIZED

Matthew 13:33 tells of the leaven which the woman mixes in three measures of meal until it is thoroughly leavened. The new leaven is the grace and faith bestowed by the Spirit. It does not leaven the whole lump at once but gently, and gradually, we become like this new leaven and eventually, a bread of God. This life, therefore, is not godliness but the process of becoming godly, not health but getting well, not being but becoming, not rest but exercise. We are not now what we shall be, but we are on the way. The process is not yet finished, but it is actively going on. This is not the goal but it is the right road. At present everything does not gleam and sparkle, but everything is being cleansed.   Martin Luther[52]

In the previous section, we considered "justification"—what God does to save humanity in Christ. We now speak of "sanctification"—what saved humanity experiences in the Holy Spirit. In the words of Orthodox theologian, Vladimir Lossky, "The church is already the Body of Christ, but she is not yet 'the fulness of Him who filleth all in all' (Eph. 1:23). The work of Christ is consummated; the work of the Holy Spirit is waiting for accomplishment."[53]

Through Christ's victory, we have been saved from sin and death; but, for what? It is never so easy to describe the conditions of peace as to describe the warfare by which the peace was won. Yet, it is here that the relation between justification and *theosis* becomes most clear.

Orthodox professor John Meyendorff has written, "the whole Greek patristic notion of 'participation in divine life,' of deification, is the real *content* of soteriology."[54] Soteriology (says Swedish Lutheran, Lars Thunberg), "in its widest and proper sense, is never concerned only for that aspect of salvation that consists in man's liberation from his sinfulness. It is the doctrine (and the mystery) of man's perfection in deification and, through man, the doctrine of the fulfilment of the destiny of the whole cosmos."[55]

Orthodox writer Georgios Mantzaridis clearly specifies that destiny: "The bliss of the faithful does not lie in the attaining of incorruptibility but in the full and lasting enjoyment of communion with God."[56] Finnish Lutheran theologian, Tuomo Mannermaa, agrees, pointing out that in Luther's understanding Christ is not only the "favor" of God (i.e., the forgiveness of sins and the repeal of God's wrath) but also the "gift" of God (i.e., God present in the fullness of his being).[57]

By participation in the church, Christians are being divinized, for they participate in the body of Christ. In Lutheran terms, the universal spiritual priesthood of all the baptized—the people of God—are sanctified as well as justified by the means of grace. Clergy and laity alike are to daily repent their sins, receive forgiveness and the gifts of the Spirit in the Word and Sacraments, and "thank, praise, serve, and obey" God (the words are from the Small Catechism of Martin Luther). In Orthodox terms,

> according to Palamas, the deification of human nature was accomplished for the first time in the person of Christ. . . . Christ's human nature became the vessel for uncreated divine energy, and henceforth communicates this grace in the Holy Spirit to all believers. Man is reborn through the sacrament of baptism, becomes one flesh with Christ through communion in His deified body, and so participates in His new life and becomes a citizen of the heavenly kingdom. By reason of his

unbreakable bond with the source of all true life, he no longer fears death nor directs his life under the shadow of its threat. . . . His main concern during earthly life is to preserve perpetual communion with God through prayer and sacramental life.[58]

In both traditions, the source of one's new life in God is the liturgical and sacramental life of the church.[59]

Communion with God has been the spiritual aim of all the saints,[60] for this world as well as the next.

The deification or *theosis* of the creature will be realized in its fullness only in the age to come, after the resurrection of the dead. This deifying union has, nevertheless, to be fulfilled ever more and more even in this present life, through the transformation of our corruptible and depraved nature and by its adaptation to eternal life.[61]

"As Maximos the Confessor shows it best, communion with the Logos is precisely the *natural state* of true humanity. Man is truly man when he participates in divine life and realizes in himself the image and likeness of God, and this participation in no way diminishes his authentically human existence, human energy and will."[62]

Similarly, confidence in the sufficiency of justification by grace alone by no means results in an unorthodox or uncatholic reduction in Christian faith and life, but rather, since the Christian is thereby set free from anxiety over salvation, permits a full flowering of spirit and activity. Indeed, while faith is no part of the means or cause of salvation, it points (no less than *theosis*) to the content and result of salvation. In his great commentary on Galatians,[63] Luther wrote:

If it is true faith, it is a sure trust and firm acceptance in the heart. It takes hold of Christ in such a way that Christ is the object of faith, or rather not the object but, so to speak, the One who is *present in the faith itself*. . . . The Christ who is grasped by faith and who *lives in the heart* is the true Christian righteousness, on account of which God counts us righteous and grants us eternal life [italics mine].[64]

Neither Luther nor Saint Paul were antinomians in their emphasis on the sole efficacy of faith for justification. While righteousness cannot be achieved by works, faith naturally issues in love (Gal. 5:6). Luther insisted that "the gospel is powerful enough to transform the righteousness of faith into a righteousness of love, . . . moving the sinful creature from egocentric self-righteousness to unselfish love of the neighbor in need."[65]

> In his wonderful essay *On Good Works* [*WA* VI, 202–276; *LW* 44:21–114], Luther declared that it is just like telling one who is sick: Get well first, and then you will also have strength to use your arms and legs. How nonsensical it would be on the part of the patient to maintain that he had been told that he need no longer use his members! After he has regained his strength, he will move them automatically and voluntarily, and this will no longer be a hardship for him but will be his joy and his most natural life. This is also the story of faith. Faith means health through God. And then an active life, a life of good works, follows as self-evidently as a healthy person moves his limbs.[66]

Thus, while such goodness as may be evident in the world is not evidence for Christian improvement toward the achievement of salvation, it does represent the in-breaking of the abundant life of the kingdom of God—beauty, truth, and goodness coming to light, even through sinners. In the Lutheran Confessions, good works are even declared to be meritorious, "not for the forgiveness of sins, grace, and justification (for we obtain these only by faith), but for other spiritual and physical rewards in this life and in that which is to come."[67] Article VI of the Augsburg Confession (entitled "The New Obedience") declares that "faith is bound to bring forth good fruits";[68] and, as the epigraph at the head of this section vividly illustrates, Luther saw the Christian life as "the process of becoming godly."

Thus, Lutheran thought is seen to be entirely compatible with the Orthodox perception that salvation involves growth into God, beginning in this present life. "Since Gregory of Nyssa," according to John Meyendorff, "the destiny of men is viewed, in Greek patristic thought, as an ascent in the knowledge of God" while "sin consists precisely in a self-affirmation of man in an illusory independence."[69] In a memorable passage, Vladimir Lossky offers a glimpse of a life yielded to and ascending in the knowledge and love of God: "To participate in the divinity of the Son, in the communal divinity of the Trinity, is to be deified, to be penetrated by divinity—just as the red-hot iron in the fire is penetrated by the heat of the fire—allowing the beauty of the inexpressible nature of

81

the Trinity to shine in us."[70] Similarly, commenting on Gal. 2:20 ("it is no longer I who live; yet not I, but it is Christ who lives in me"), Luther wrote: "This 'I' Paul rejects; for 'I,' as a person distinct from Christ, belongs to death and hell. . . . Indeed, Christ Himself is the life that I now live. In this way, therefore, Christ and I are one."[71]

As we have seen, "faith" is the word most often used by Lutherans to refer to this participation in and penetration by the divine life. In the New Testament, "faith" often denotes a relationship with God that the Christian has in this life as an "earnest" of the life to come. In Hebrews 11:1, faith is defined as "the *hypostasis* of things hoped for" (perhaps the King James Version translates it best as "substance"). Faith is certainly something other than and far more than "assurance" (as the RSV and the NRSV give it). *Hypostasis* means a specifically existent reality; and faith is definitely the reality of belonging to God now in a new and intimate relationship—not merely "assurance" that such a relationship is coming after death—a foretaste of that total transfiguration, that full *theosis*, to come.

Thus Luther can write that "the one who has faith is a completely divine man, a son of God, the inheritor of the universe. He is the victor over the world, sin, death, and the devil"; and, in a clear and unqualified affirmation of *theosis*: "Faith makes a man God."[72]

THE INTEGRATION OF JUSTIFICATION AND DEIFICATION

Even in the age to come, the saints' vision of God will not be static. "Clearly it will develop infinitely. . . . The saints, communing in the grace of God and rendered through that communion more and more able to contain the divine radiance, will receive grace upon grace from God Himself, its infinite and unfailing source."   Gregory Palamas[73]

Those who are engaged in the quest for Christian unity can find courage and zest in Jesus' promise that the Spirit "will guide you into all the truth" and "declare to you the things that are to come" (John 16:13)—courage, because the promise is unqualified; zest, because new discoveries clearly lie ahead.

God's manner of effecting new and deeper relationships (from marriage to the incarnation) makes it clear that effective ecumenical relations depend upon reconciling love. Theological insights that have developed in diverse traditions must be integrated without violating the integrity of those traditions. However, the mutual submission of love in a true marriage often leads to the alteration or abandonment of some former ways as well as the disclosure and realization of heretofore undreamed-of potentialities.

Lutherans and Orthodox are working toward the integration of traditions that reveal a gratifyingly high degree of correspondence. To be sure, each tradition includes aspects that are problematic for the other. Some Orthodox statements express a synergism that Lutherans perceive as a confusion of justification and sanctification, reflecting an inadequate distinction between law and gospel. According to Timothy Ware, "Man, while he cannot 'merit' salvation, must certainly work for it, since 'faith without works is dead' ";[74] and, "In his own person, Christ showed what the true 'likeness of God' is, and through His redeeming and victorious sacrifice, He set that likeness once again within man's reach."[75] According to Maximos Confessor, "Our salvation finally depends on our own will."[76]

Aware that the last statement would strike many readers as outright heresy, Jaroslav Pelikan explains that "the antithesis between Pelagianism and Augustinianism was not a part of Maximos's thought."[77] That disadvantage, however, is not shared by the theological heirs of Maximos (and Augustine) who, in current ecumenical dialogues, can deal with such apparent stumbling blocks as opportunities for refinement of thought and expression.

This study of the Lutheran emphasis on justification in light of the Orthodox emphasis on deification has revealed that, while Lutherans speak of "faith" and Orthodox speak of *theosis*, both understand the Christian's hope as "belonging to God." The Lutheran concern to specify the *means* of salvation and the Orthodox concern for its *meaning* are two insights into the one unspeakably wonderful reality that God, by grace alone, for the sake of Christ alone, has forgiven our sins and given us everlasting salvation.

Joint theological work toward the integration of these insights has the potential for mutual enrichment and renewal. Above all, such efforts, made in response to Jesus' prayer "that they may all be one . . . so that the world may believe" (John 17:21), could result in a more faithful and effective proclamation of the gospel for the salvation of the world.

4

Human Participation in the Divine-Human Dialogue

THE HUMAN CONDITION

The Lutheran Confessions do not articulate a formal doctrine of creation, but the references that exist speak of creation as being good. Essentially these explain the opening clause in the creed, "Creator of heaven and earth, and of all things, visible and invisible."

> Our attention is directed immediately to God and his deed, and the idea is precluded that the creatureliness of created things is a quality of this world which has reality apart from God and his action. God is the Lord who was in eternity before all things and who in the beginning of things called into existence the things that do not exist.[1]

Human life was created possessing both the *imago dei* and the *similitudo dei*, that is, qualities of moral perfection that reflected God's nature, including reason and free will. After the fall humans retained their status as creatures of God in that God continues to preserve and protect humanity, and continues to create and preserve his creation. Luther in his Large Catechism rehearses all the activities of God in giving and sustaining life, "all this is comprehended in the word, 'creator.' "[2]

Humans fell into sin from primordial goodness. The struggle to diagnose sin has led Christians to speculate on the origin of sin. The Lutheran Confessions say very little about sin's origins other than to repeat the imagery of Genesis 3 and the fact of the inevitability and universality of sin as expressed by Saint Paul in Rom. 5:12. Nonetheless, the question remains crucial if we are to avoid Manichaeism which assumes an evil force equal to God (Satan?), or suggests that God is the source of sin, as nothing comes into being without him—we know that he is good. Lutherans have no answer to this perennial puzzle other than to insist that sin entered the world through human free will, and that ultimately humans are responsible for sin. "The consensus of Christian reflection resists any reference to the demonic that would compromise the reality of human responsibility."[3]

Whatever we make of the tempter's role in the origin of sin, in the primeval account the human pair come to bear the consequences of their own deeds. The Formula of Concord speaks of the source of sin as "the devil and man's wicked and perverse will."[4] Luther's Large Catechism says: "When we were created by God the Father, and had received from him all kinds of good things, the devil came and led us into disobedience, sin, death, and all evil."[5] But this explanation continues by claiming that it is we who accordingly "lay under God's wrath and displeasure, doomed to eternal damnation, as we had deserved." Here human responsibility is intact. Human sin occurs through external temptation, not through external coercion.

Likewise, the question of the transmission of sin remains unsolved. Some Lutherans have leaned toward the traducianism of Tertullian ("that which is born of flesh is flesh") yet they reject the Augustinian notion of "concupiscence" as the source of sin, that is, the act of conception is itself tainted. The locus classicus remains Rom. 5:12: "Therefore just as sin came into the world through one man, and death came through sin, and so death spread to all because all have sinned," together with Ps. 51:5, "Indeed, I was born guilty, a sinner when my mother conceived me."

Regardless of the origin of sin or its transmission, neither being a settled issue, it remains empirically demonstrable that all human beings share in the condition we call sin. Jaroslav Pelikan has observed, "the statistical regularity with which men who supposedly faced Adam's possibilities always made Adam's choice."[6] The Augsburg Confession states:

> It is also taught among us that since the fall of Adam, all men who are born according to the course of nature are conceived and born in sin. That is, all men are full of evil lust and inclinations from their mothers' wombs and are unable by nature

to have true fear of God and true faith in God. Moreover, this inborn sickness and hereditary sin is truly sin and condemns to the eternal wrath of God all those who are not born again through baptism and the Holy Spirit. Rejected in this connection are the Pelagians and others who deny that original sin is sin, for they hold that natural man is made righteous by his own power, thus disparaging the sufferings and merits of Christ.[7]

This presents us with the enigma of original sin, or the sin of our origin. The earliest evidence for this is in Tertullian, but Cyprian is the clearest witness from antiquity, and he bases his doctrine on the practice of infant baptism.[8] Ambrose finds support for original sin in the doctrine of the virgin birth of Christ. Augustine maintained that "what we hold is the true, the truly Christian, and the catholic faith as was handed down of old through the sacred Scriptures, and so retained and preserved by our fathers to this very time, in which these men (Pelagians) have attempted to overthrow it."[9] Although Origen acknowledges a form of original sin—"It is for this reason that the church has received from the apostles the tradition of giving baptism to infants . . . for no one is free from sin even though his life has been for only one day"[10]—yet he sits lightly on the idea. Most of the Eastern fathers either decline to comment on the question or, like Theodore of Mopsuestia, are opposed to it.

The Lutheran Confessions do not elaborate on original sin, nor do they distinguish between it and the actual sins done by individuals themselves. Rather, they stress our solidarity as humans in sharing a sinful nature.

> The will to commit or omit sin does not begin with a clean slate. Biblical writers recognize a "continuity in sin." . . . Selves do not exist in insulated tubes of being; they exist in relationships, and it is those relationships which make up the world. The sin and sins of selves enter the world to yield a solidarity in sin. No self begins with a clean slate. It is born into this world with its racism, sexism, profit-oriented economy, consumerism, etc.[11]

And yet humans remain responsible. "The fact that the sinful condition of the present generation has resulted from the perverted direction of an earlier one in no sense does away with the responsibility of the former group."[12]

A familiar biblical refrain is "There is no one who does not sin" (1 Kgs. 8:46; 2 Chr. 6:36). "There is no one who is righteous, not even one" (Rom. 3:10). Even Noah and Job who were said to be righteous were so because of their relationship with God. "It is not a matter of separate transgressions, nor simply of the failure of one generation, but of a deep-seated inability to obey, indeed of a resistance to God (which made itself manifest on the very day that Israel came into being)."[13] We therefore affirm both the inevitability and the universality of the sinful condition, and it is in this light that original sin should be understood. "Sin and original sin are interchangeable concepts. . . . The whole weight of the numerous doctrinal declarations about original sin is forthwith concentrated on OUR sin."[14] The Confessions do not develop a doctrine of the imputation of Adam's sin to his progeny. Rather, the fact of the universal relationship of all individuals in sin results in a community of sin. Every infant is born into this community. Hence, we originate in sin and continue in this solidarity with all humans. This is the meaning of original sin. Lutherans have not followed Augustine to his unacceptable conclusion that unbaptized infants are condemned.[15] Rather, they emphasize the need for a child to enter the community of grace as soon as possible in order to grow in faith toward God. Baptism was intended for those who will physically and spiritually grow and mature; it was not intended as the last rites.

The human condition from birth onward is that of sinner. What is the nature of sin? Basically, it is to be against God, or to be God oneself in place of God. Luther wrote, "Man cannot of his nature desire that God might be God; on the contrary, he desires that he himself might be God, and that God might not be God."[16] This was the primordial temptation, "Ye shall be as gods." Luther expands on this in his explanation of the first commandment in the Large Catechism. "Man's whole heart and confidence should be placed in God alone and in no one else. . . . Everyone has . . . set up a god of his own."[17] If one can "keep" this first commandment, one can "keep" the entire law. The Confessions point to the deep-seated and all-pervasive sickness of sin. It is more than mere failure, or mere ignorance, or mere weakness. It is a sickness unto death. It is: "a deep, wicked, abominable, bottomless, inscrutable, and inexpressible corruption of his [or her] entire nature in all its powers, especially of the highest and foremost powers of the soul in mind and heart and will."[18]

Therefore humans have lost the image of God despite being creatures of God. There is predicated of humanity "a complete lack or absence of the original concreated righteousness of paradise or of the image of God according to which man [or woman] was originally created in truth, holiness, and righteousness."[19] Fallen humanity has lost God's image, and this can be recaptured only through regeneration, when we are "changed into his likeness," that is, we acquire the true knowledge of God.[20] Sin also results in a loss of the knowledge of God. It is "such faults as ignorance of God, contempt of God, lack of the fear of God and of trust in him, inability to love him."[21]

Joseph Sittler, one of this generation's foremost Lutheran theologians, comments on original sin:

> The term original sin remains as a kind of pail which we've drained of the old literal statements and refilled with quite new interpretations. The doctrine meant to point to the gravity, the universality, and the demonic results of evil. And the language was a way of stating this. But we no longer buy the old notion of biological transmission or try to have a system of inheritance. The notion of "original" means profound—trans-individual, way back and deep down. The analogy of evil has changed, but the reality hasn't lessened.[22]

Liturgically we find reflection of our sinful state in the Lutheran services. The Sacrament of Holy Baptism begins with this exhortation:

> In Holy Baptism our heavenly Father liberates us from sin and death by joining us to the death and resurrection of our Lord Jesus Christ. We are born children of a fallen humanity; in the waters of Holy Baptism we are reborn children of God and inheritors of the church which is the body of Christ. As we live with Him and with His people, we grow in faith, love, and obedience to the will of God.[23]

> By the baptism of His own death and resurrection your beloved Son has set us free from the bondage to sin and death, and has opened the way to the joy and freedom of everlasting life.[24]

The regular Sunday Order of Confession begins, "We confess that we are in bondage to sin and cannot free ourselves." And yet we remain God's creatures, and as such retain some reminiscences of God's image. It is crucial to recognize that the Confessions do not speak of sin as integral to human nature, but as contingent. Sin is not "substance" but *accidens*. Sin was "added" to humans from external sources.[25] Human nature "even after the Fall . . . is and remains a creature of God."[26] "Scripture testifies not only that God created human nature before the Fall, but also that after the fall human nature is God's creature and handiwork."[27] People have retained a "dim spark" of the knowledge of God, sufficient to be aware of God's law and of the natural knowledge of God. They are not totally ignorant of God, but are ignorant of God's true nature and are without saving knowledge. Humanity has sufficient knowledge of God's law to attempt its fulfillment (Rom. 1:19), but following this law leads only to despair. If sin is to be "against God," sufficient knowledge of God must be present in order to be against him, or to hate him, or to deny him. Thus it is incorrect to speak of humanity's "total depravity" or as human nature being sinful in its essence in the Augustinian sense. Therefore it seems that Luther's idea of losing the image of God entirely cannot be upheld. Humanity retains a basic knowledge of right and wrong, the use of reason in matters of justice, and some sense of God's existence through natural knowledge. Nevertheless it can be said that Lutherans espouse a basically pessimistic view of humanity in the sight of God, more so, it appears, than the Orthodox churches, the Roman church, or many Protestant communions.

This brings us to the problematic issue of free will. Luther's most extensive statement is *On the Bondage of the Will*, his longest treatise, written in 1525 to answer Erasmus' *On the Freedom of the Will*. But earlier, in the Heidelberg Disputations of 1518, Luther had already outlined his position on the will, which was condemned two years later by a papal bull. Basically Luther denied that unregenerate humanity possesses free will. "After the fall of Adam, free-will is a mere expression; whenever it acts in character, it commits mortal sin."[28] Here Luther follows the example of Peter Lombard, who found humanity totally bereft of free will, whereas Erasmus was in debt to Aquinas, who taught that humanity retained some freedom of choice, or else there could be no responsibility. This is not to say that we cannot make free choices in everyday decisions, or in marrying or having children. In his *Exposition on Genesis* Luther wrote:

> We have, of course, in a certain sense a free-will in those things which are under us. For the divine mandate has constituted us lords of the fishes of the sea, of the fowls of the air, and of

the beasts of the field. . . . We enjoy the food and the other useful things they supply. But in things pertaining to God, in matters which are above us, man has no free-will at all. He is in reality as clay in the hand of the potter, clay which is merely worked on by power from without and is not active in itself. Here, then, we choose nothing; we do nothing. On the contrary, we are chosen; we are prepared; we are regenerated; we receive, as Isaiah says: "Thou art our Potter, we are Thy clay." (Isa. 64:8)[29]

For Luther, our will is in bondage to all matters pertaining to salvation. He wrote in his explanation of the Third Article of the Apostle's Creed: "I believe that I cannot of my own reason or strength believe in Jesus Christ, my Lord, or come to him. But the Holy Spirit has called me by the Gospel, enlightened me with His gifts, sanctified and kept me in the true faith."

The Confessions echo these ideas. "In some measure our free-will is capable of living honorably or dishonorably, and this is what Scriptures call the righteousness of the law or of the flesh."[30] "But without the grace, help, and activity of the Holy Spirit man is not capable of making himself acceptable to God, of fearing God, and of believing in God with his whole heart, or of expelling inborn evil lusts from his heart."[31] What Luther and the reformers were seeking to safeguard by their insistence on the bondage of the will was the totally unilateral nature of salvation, that God's grace was the sole agent of salvation, and man was incapable of contributing to it, not even by making a "decision for Christ."

Yet humanity has the freedom of choice within the bounds of the natural orders, and can freely move about in the realm below. This includes the freedom to create great works of art, of symphonies and philosophical systems, of family and marriage, of justice and the creation of civil orders. It is only in our relationship to God that our will is under bondage.

God always judges total man . . . either the volition of a good man or bad man. Bondage of the will means in the first place that we are compelled to will as we are, and in the second place that we can never will as good people, because under God's judgement we are never good. In order to be good we would have to reflect the goodness of God within ourselves, but that exceeds our ability. The fact alone that God had to impose the law upon us proves it. . . . There would be no need for a law if we ourselves reflected the goodness of God. The law brings our sin out into the open.[32]

There is no ethical neutrality, no moment when we can freely choose to be a sinner or not to be a sinner. We cannot will as though there were no sin. We are entangled in our sin, and our will is bound. The law exists to convict us of our sin (*lex semper accusat*). By nature we are incapable of performing good works or living virtuous lives that will in any way assist us toward salvation. A person may perform "virtuous" deeds, but in the eyes of God these are nothing, and a person who places hope for some kind of salvation upon virtue is doomed to disappointment. We cannot of our own free will gain credits with God. "For I do not do the good I want, but the evil I do not want is what I do. Wretched man that I am! Who will rescue me from this body of death?" (Rom. 7:19, 24).

It is clear that in articulating the bondage of the will the Lutheran confessors were continuing a discussion that reached back to the early years of the church, that is, the tension between the inevitability of sin and the responsibility of the sinner. In their opposition to Gnostic determinism, theologians such as Justin, the Greek Apologists, and the anti-Gnostic polemicists insisted on free will. Saint Irenaeus wrote, "All men are of the same nature, able both to hold fast and do what is good, and on the other hand, having also the power to cast it from them and not do it."[33] They championed the responsibility of humans to resist the fatalism of the Gnostics and assume some degree of control over their lives. No longer could a person excuse one's behavior by saying "the devil made me do it," or the stars, or the Fates. The ideal was that of self-determination (*autexousion*). Numerous references from the Scriptures, especially from the synoptic Gospels, supported the idea that in humanity's ethical life there are moral choices to make. The clear danger in holding to this ideal apart from Saint Paul was to establish Christianity as a new moralism divorced from the need for God's grace or the saving work of Christ.

After Saint Augustine, the Western church gave primary attention to the inevitability of sin, with its corresponding flirtation with fatalism and Manichaeism. With the total passivity of humanity required by holding to the bondage of the will, the concept of predestination appeared to be a logical conclusion. Saint Augustine did not flinch from the latter, which the second council of Orange (A.D. 529) rejected. Much of the history of Western Christian thought from Saint Augustine to Luther had to do with the tension between inevitability and responsibility. Without freedom of choice, there can be no responsibility. But if humanity is responsible alone for virtue (salvation?) what need is there for a savior? Or if the savior is merely an assistant or a guide for the weak, is this not what Pelagius advocated? How shall we reconcile, "For by grace you have been saved through faith, and this is not your own doing; it is the gift of God" (Eph. 2:8), with freedom and responsibility? The reformers believed they had safely steered through this Scylla and Charybdis, though there was considerable tension among Lutherans on these issues, resulting in the not entirely satisfactory and sometimes incomprehensible Formula of Concord of 1577.

HUMAN RECEPTION OF GOD'S PROMISE

The foregoing account of man's passivity being acted upon by God's grace in order to "effect" a conversion assumes a cause/effect relationship. When God is granted ultimate causal efficacy, the human recipient becomes the wholly passive object. When humans are given a share in the "cause" of salvation, God's ultimate priority is jeopardized. Lutherans discarded cause/effect categories in favor of the Confessions' use of "promise" as gospel. Pre-Reformation Western theology consistently understood divine-human relations in causal terms. Thus Aquinas, following Augustine, spoke of God's prior action in moving the will to believe as "operating grace" and of our secondary but not necessary (i.e., automatic) involvement in that willing as "cooperating grace." Robert Jenson has analyzed the consequences of this cooperative causal process:

> When the saving relationship between God and believers is understood as the causality of one substance on another, salvation is necessarily understood as a process. Whatever may be the virtues of such descriptions . . . they are theological catastrophes. For if salvation is thus understood as a process between two agents, then unless I am to be a mere spectator of my own life, there must be points in the process where the move is up to me and where the next stage will not occur unless I make the move.[34]

The Lutheran reformers responded to this incipient works-righteousness by redefining grace as promise. The primary expression is found in Melanchthon's Apology to the Augsburg Confession:

> All Scriptures should be divided into these two chief doctrines, the law and the promises. In some places it presents the law.

In others it presents the promise of Christ. This it does either when it promises that the Messiah will come and promises the forgiveness of sins, justification, and eternal life for his sake, or when, in the New Testament, the Christ who came promises forgiveness of sins, justification, and eternal life.[35]

Melanchthon continually relates promise to the blessings of forgiveness, justification, and eternal life. Promise here is not limited to future benefits, though it includes them, but the promise already grants the blessings it pledges. The promise bestows forgiveness and reconciliation in the act of promising. "The Gospel is, strictly speaking, the promise of forgiveness of sins and justification because of Christ."[36] Promise underscores the unconditional offer of salvation—not conditioned by human response. Thus the causal connection is broken.

This promise is not conditional upon our merits but offers the forgiveness of sins and justification freely. If the promise were conditional upon our merits and the law, which we never keep, it would follow that the promise is useless. Since we obtain justification through a free promise, however, it follows that we cannot justify ourselves. Otherwise why would a promise be necessary?[37]

In exploring this concept Ronald Thiemann refers to the eucharistic prayer (Great Thanksgiving) to illustrate the promise as continuing narrative.[38] "Through Abraham you promised to bless all nations," and "through the prophets you renewed your promise"—implying God as actor and church as recipient. God and humanity are in relation to one another, starting from the basic conviction that "in Christ God was reconciling the world to himself, not counting their trespasses against them, and entrusting the message of reconciliation to us" (2 Cor. 5:19). That message of reconciliation is God's promise, which binds God and humanity together while granting absolute priority to God's initiating action.

Promise is a relational category that implies both a speaker and a hearer. The hearer merely acknowledges the promise, but the acknowledgment does not constitute the promise. Nor should the act of recognizing the promise be equated with faith. Faith requires a further movement of the heart and spirit in response to the promise. Faith is not a work that I must perform in order to make the promise effective. The promise is not conditional upon faith or unfaith. The promise is "received" by faith in the Promisor, but that faith is prompted by the Promisor and the promise. Faith is "no mere historical knowledge, but the firm acceptance of God's offer," the certain and firm trust in the heart, when with my whole heart I regard the promise of God as certain and true, through which there is offered, without my merit, the forgiveness of sins, grace, and all blessing, through Christ the mediator.[39] To have faith means to want and accept (*velle et accipere*) the promised offer.[40] What does "to will" imply? Justus Jonas, a reformer, suggests, "It is not my doing, not my granting or giving, not my working or preparing, but that the heart comforts itself and is altogether confident that God bestows on us and gives us, and not we him."[41] The act of volition is not a human deed but the longing desire and wish that is aroused and appeased by the promise. This daring reliance and clinging to the promise is the extent of our human activity, but it cannot be defined as a human work.

Faith is confidence (*fiducia*), that is, "assurance that God is gracious to us, and we have confidence in God and in his promise."[42] The Confessions not only say that God imputes Christ's righteousness to the sinner, but also that "God will regard and reckon this faith as righteousness."[43] It is the very righteousness by which we are accounted righteous before God."[44]

All illustrations are limited, but it may be helpful to offer the paradigm of a disobedient child. A child has been wicked through willful disobedience, i.e., breaking windows and destroying furniture. He is reminded that when the father returns home, he will be angry and will severely punish the child. The knowledge (*Lae*) evokes a sense of fear in the child, whose day becomes a nightmare of dreaded judgment. In order to assuage the father's wrath, the child tries to correct the damage and do other things that may please the father. But the boy remains uncertain of the father's reaction, which casts a pall of gloomy foreboding over his day. Then he receives the telephone call (promise) from the father who acknowledges that the child has been disobedient, but the father has determined to forgive him, and more than that, to bring gifts to the child upon returning that evening. How shall the child respond? He will be elated, euphoric, and joyful. The burden has been removed. His day is now full of eager anticipation for the father's return. He is motivated by love rather than fear of the father. He redoubles his efforts at doing things that please the father. He will no longer be destructive or do anything to further displease the father. He lives in the happy and confident freedom of knowing his father loves him and has forgiven him.

Applying this analogy to the Christian, one cannot say the child cooperated with the father's promise. It was the promise that evoked love and joy in the child. To be sure, the child may reject the promise or disbelieve it. But it cannot be said that it was an act of the child's "will" that accepted the promise. The promise itself spontaneously evoked "faith" and love. The "works" performed as a result of that "faith" are not performed under obligation or constraint (i.e., fear or law) but as a result of a relationship that has been reestablished (reconciliation). In the context of sanctification, the child's response to the father's promise is that of willingly and gladly doing those things that will please the father, i.e., becoming more like the father, or godlike. This is the human response to the divine initiative.

But the child need not rely upon his own strength or "will" to perform such good works. In Christian terms the believer has also been promised the gift of the Holy Spirit to do things that please the Father. This is clearly reflected in the Lutheran liturgy in the words of the absolution: "In the mercy of almighty God, Jesus Christ was given to die for you, and for his sake God forgives you all your sins. To those who believe in Jesus Christ *he gives the power to become the children of God and bestows on them the Holy Spirit.*"[45]

It has been suggested that the preceding illustration is too idealistic. It reflects the sense of joy and release experienced by Luther, who had suffered under a load of guilt and the fear (dread) of a just God. ("How can I find a gracious God?") Upon discovering the "promise," he experienced such a release that his entire life henceforth was imbued with a sense of ecstasy, revelling in the heady knowledge of a loving Father. But such is not the case for many Christians who may require some "guidelines" for conduct while awaiting the Father's return. (The so-called third use of the law.) More on this follows.

HUMAN RESPONSE TO GOD'S INITIATIVE

"Should we continue to sin in order that grace may abound? By no means! How can we who died to sin still live in it?" (Rom. 6:1, 2). For Lutherans, justification means the end of the law (doing good out of fear of punishment, or for a reward, or to "justify" oneself). It means the death of the old and resurrection of the new in faith, as a result of Holy Baptism and the gift of the Holy Spirit. Good works proceed because through justification the sinner is good (*justus*) and the works result because the tree is good. The goodness of the tree results in good fruit; it is not the good fruit that produces a good tree. Faith naturally produces good works. Luther was faulted as was Saint Paul, for fostering an ethical permissiveness that could lead to moral anarchy. This is not only to misread Luther, but in empirical terms the intervening four centuries have not shown Lutherans to be demonstrably below the moral standards of fellow Christians. Neither has the same evidence indicated a greater euphoria or joy on the part of Lutherans. We have said that justification makes the sinner "good." This is not merely in a make-believe sense, i.e., that the sinner actually remains "bad" but God simply overlooks it, for faith is a divine work in us and changes us. There is an ontological change in Baptism that brings with it the indwelling Christ and the very real presence of the Holy Spirit. Luther writes:

> Faith is a divine work in us which changes us and births us anew out of God (John 1:13), and kills the old Adam, makes us into entirely different people from the heart, soul, mind and all powers, and brings the Holy Spirit with it. Oh, it is a living, busy, active, mighty thing, this faith, so it is impossible that it should not do good. . . . It does not ask if good works should be done, but before one asks, has done them and is always active. Whoever, though, does not do such work is a faithless person, peeking and poking about for faith and good works not knowing what either faith or good works are, who putters and patters many words about faith and good works.[46]

Luther spoke of the spontaneity and freedom with which works flow forth from faith. His words, *quellende Liebe*, mean a "bubbling over," "springing forth" as from a spring. The point is that love bubbles forth from itself because of faith.[47]

In discussing this spontaneity, Gerhard Forde cautions against equating it with the "voice of conscience" or the "moral law within" or the "human moral autonomy" of Kant or that doing may improve one's self-image. Rather, "the spring is the Word of God, the justification given for Jesus' sake. That 'spring' alone purifies the heart from the lust for either vice or virtue, so that good works will flow forth."[48] The Word is spoken; faith hears. From that good works flow.

We have just said that faith frees us from both vice and virtue. By this is meant that we are no longer under the law of compulsion, the demands of virtue, because the law no longer controls us. Only faith and hope and love guide us. Hearing the divine declaration alone will set us free over against good works. The movement of faith to good works must be a movement of freedom. If not, we become prisoners of our works. We look at them to find our being, our status. Luther writes, "When you look to what you have done you have already lost the name of Christian. It is indeed true that one should do good works, help others, advise and give, but no one is called a Christian for that, and is not a Christian for that."[49] Good deeds do not make a Christian. It is only faith that makes a believer. When one invites a nonbeliever to "join" church, and the response is, "I can be just as good a person outside Christianity as within it," an appropriate theological rejoinder might be, "What has that to do with it? You are invited to faith in Christ and to worship him—not to strenuous feats of virtue." The definition of a Christian may be expressed better in terms of the worship of God in Christ as a result of faith and within the community of faith. Luther writes:

Making pious people is not the business of the Gospel but only making Christians. It is more a matter of being Christian than being pious. Someone may well be pious but not a Christian. A Christian does not know how to say anything about his piety. He does not find anything good or pious in it; should he desire to become pious he will have to look to some other and foreign piousness.[50]

The Augsburg Confession echoes this when it states:

Good works should and must be done, not that we are to rely on them to earn grace but that we may do God's will and glorify him. It is always faith alone that apprehends grace and forgiveness of sins. When through faith the Holy Spirit is given, the heart is moved to do good works.[51]

This was the focus of attention in Luther's *Freedom of A Christian* with its well-known opening statement: "A Christian is a perfectly free lord of all, subject to none. A Christian is a perfectly dutiful servant of all, subject to all."[52] The first clause refers to one's freedom from rules; the second clause refers to the way in which one expresses faith and love to God. To the person who says, "If faith does all things . . . we will take our ease and do no works," Luther responds: "You wicked man, not so. A man cannot be idle. He is compelled to do many good works."[53] Among such works are feeding the hungry, giving money for the poor, and devoting oneself to the welfare of others, whether they be friend or foe, and not in the hope of gratitude or reward.

Yet the Scriptures have much to say about rewards to those who do God's will. The Confessions speak in this way:

> We teach that rewards are offered and promised to the works of believers. We teach that good works are meritorious—not that they merit forgiveness of sins, grace and justification, for these we obtain by faith alone, but that they merit other bodily and spiritual rewards in this life and in the life to come, because Saint Paul says, "Each one will receive a reward in proportion to his labor (1 Cor. 3:8)."[54]

Is this too idealistic? Can anyone love with such perfect agape? Does not the child require admonitions not to break any more windows? Is not it helpful for the lover to be reminded to observe a birthday? And what of the Decalogue, or all the paranetic material in the Gospels? Are not these useful to point the way of Christian sanctification and walking in newness of life? Here we must speak of the simultaneity of being both righteous and a sinner, *simul justus et peccator*. Even a post-baptismal person remains a sinner while also being righteous through faith. To the extent that one remains a sinner one is reminded of a need for grace for the use of the law. The state of righteousness and sinfulness remains 100 percent until death. A person does not increase in sanctification to the point of being entirely holy. It is not a gradual process of catching up to the *totus justus*, as though imputed righteousness is a temporary loan given to cover lack of capital until one has earned enough by oneself. Rather, following Wilfried Joest, there is a growth, to be sure, but one of grace rather than works. "The movement drives toward fulfillment when by the power of the coming reality the *totus peccator* shall finally die completely and by grace alone be turned totally to love the God who gives it. . . . The growth is a growth of grace."[55] It is not that we become less sinful, but that we grow in divine likeness. The commands of the Scriptures are such as to show us our sin in failing to live up to them. Lutherans have not been in agreement on the nature of such commands. They are law, to be sure, but of what kind? Of the uses of the law we speak of the first, which is natural law common to all societies ("Thou shalt not kill") written in the human heart (Rom. 1:18ff.), which serves as a mirror to show us our shortcomings. By measuring ourselves against it we see how far we have missed the mark. The so-called "third use of the law" is to act as a guide in our life of sanctification.

That growth is external in that human beings will remain sinners until death. Sins are symptoms of our nature as sinners, and no matter how few sins a person commits, one remains a sinner in need of God's grace.

In the context of Eastern Orthodox theology, Gerhard Forde finds greater affinities in Lutheranism with the former than with late medieval thought or its contemporary expressions. The reformers understood passages of the Scripture that refer to divinization as the indwelling Christ who progressively, by grace, "sanctifies" the believer and so increasingly brings him or her to holiness. Also, the Orthodox view "stresses the radical newness that comes through participation in the divine, the creative 'energies' unleashed for salvation in the resurrection of the crucified one. The human person is assumed into the internal life of God."[56]

One's growth in Christ is related to one's exposure to the Word of God, i.e., the proclamation of the gospel and the use of the sacraments. It is only by living with this Word that a person's faith can be nourished and grace abound. Grace is understood to mean the divine/human relationship and not the "matter" of dynamic "stuff" of the scholastics. The Word of God comes to us in the proclamation of law and gospel and in the sacraments. We shall briefly speak of the sacraments in terms of human response to God's initiative, and of proclamation under the next section.

The sacraments are not only "signs" of Christ's presence, but they also convey his grace and love. The Augsburg Confession states:

> It is taught among us that the sacraments were instituted not only to be signs by which people may be identified outwardly as Christians, but they are signs and testimonies of God's will toward us for the purpose of awakening and strengthening our faith. For this reason they require faith, and they are rightly used when they are received in faith and for the purpose of strengthening faith.[57]

The sacraments are those rites instituted by Christ himself that offer forgiveness under visible signs, or serve as visible word (*verbum visibile*), "a sort of picture of the Word (*pictura verbi*)," "a painting whereby the same is signified as is proclaimed through the Word."[58] They are external signs that have God's command and the promise of grace. The Lutheran church has never declared the definite number of sacraments. The Confessions speak of three, including Confession after Baptism and Eucharist.[59] These are given by God's initiative and necessitate a human response, that is, a sacrificial dimension.

In Holy Baptism we have been adopted into God's family, which is the realm of grace. All sanctification flows from Baptism, as Luther wrote: "(Baptism) signifies that the old Adam in us should by daily contrition and repentance be drowned and die with all sins and evil lusts and, again, a new man daily come forth and arise who shall live before God in righteousness and purity forever."[60] The Augsburg Confession speaks of Baptism: "It is taught among us that baptism is necessary and that grace is offered through it. Children too should be baptized, for in baptism they are committed to God and become acceptable to him."[61] Baptism is into Christ's death and resurrection, it incorporates the believer into Christ's body, and in the chrismation seals the candidate with the Holy Spirit forever. The Lutheran liturgy has restored Luther's "flood prayer" to the rubrics that include the typology of the waters of creation, the flood, and the crossing of the Jordan as signs of life coming from death. Baptism individualizes salvation not only through the giving of a name but more significantly of the name Christian. The objective nature of Baptism, which does not depend upon one's subjective emotions or even upon one's decision, was a great comfort to Luther. He recalled how doubts about God's grace had entered his heart, and he was reassured with the recollection, "I am baptized." "Whenever your heart wants to grow timid and fearful because of sin, call to mind the covenant God has made with you in baptism at the beginning of your life and cling to the Word and sacred sacrament."[62]

In the Eucharist the Christian receives Christ's true (*vere*) body and blood into him or herself. It is a sign of the promise, it is forgiveness, it is God's presence, it is (in the words of Ignatius of Antioch) the medicine of immortality. "What the Supper signifies and effects is the fellowship of all the saints. This fellowship consists in this, that all the spiritual possessions of Christ and his saints are shared with . . . him who receives this sacrament.[63] The Eucharist may be understood and expounded under these five motifs: (1) "remembrance" (anamnesis) is that by which we not only recall but make present again Christ's saving act, not only in time past but also in the present for us; (2) "fellowship" (*koinonia*) with God and with fellow believers in time past, present, and future, as we sing in the liturgy, "therefore with angels and archangels and all the company of heaven"; (3) "thanksgiving" (*eucharistia*) is that which our Lord did in instituting this sacrament; he took bread and gave thanks; (4) "confession and forgiveness" is associated with the Eucharist, not only as a gift but also as preparation for its reception. "This is my body, given for you," includes the promise of forgiveness, reconciliation, and unity with Christ. Ordinarily the liturgy opens with the confession of sins, exceptions being made on festival days when opportunity for confession may be offered at a time prior to the liturgy; (5) "anticipation" (eschatology) is also integral to the Eucharist. We sing of it as "a foretaste of the feast to come," and remind ourselves of Christ's promise that he would not eat or drink of it until we are gathered together in his Father's home. "For as often as you eat this bread and drink the cup, you proclaim the Lord's death until he comes" (1 Cor. 11:26). It is a sign of the heavenly banquet toward which we are tending, and a comfort in times of mourning as well as a foundation of our hope.

Of this sacrament the Augsburg Confession states: "It is taught among us that the true body and blood of Christ are really present in the supper of our Lord under the forms of bread and wine and are there distributed and received."[64] The reformers restored Communion in "both kinds," i.e., bread and wine, as the norm. In answer to their critics, the reformers insisted, "Without boasting it is manifest that the Mass is observed among us with greater devotion and more earnestness than among our opponents."[65]

Earlier it was said that the sacraments are both sacramental and sacrificial, that is, they involve both a divine and human dimension. Inasmuch as we are concerned here with human response, it is appropriate to speak of the sacraments as sacrifice. The Augsburg Confession defines a sacrifice as "an action or work we give to God to do him honor." It continues by saying, "(one) kind of sacrifice is the eucharistic sacrifice, which does not merit remission of sins, but is offered by those who have already been reconciled as a thank-offering for the forgiveness of sins that they have received or for other benefits that they have from God's hand."[66] Lutherans have always understood the sacraments to be a sacrifice of praise and thanksgiving to God. "Do this" or "baptize" is a command for us to do something, to act something out, and as such is a human, not a divine, activity. Robert Jenson writes:

> Whatever we will say about the Eucharist as a sacrament, as God's act toward us, it will not be prompted by trying to pretend that the Eucharist is not also our act toward God. Indeed, in a sense the Eucharist is first our deed, for we are the ones who gather the elements and bring them. Just as the

preacher's sermon is a pure message of grace, and so a sacrament, it is also the result of his own sweat and prayer, and so a sacrifice. But God makes it to be God's address, and so a word of grace.[67]

The sacrificial aspects of the Eucharist are understood in the offertory prayer, "we *offer* with joy and gladness . . . with them (gifts) we *offer* ourselves,"[68] together with the terminology that still refers to the focal point of worship as an "altar" as well as a table.

Likewise Baptism includes sacrificial aspects: parallelisms between it and circumcision (Col. 2:11-12; 2 Cor. 1:22); the identification of baptism with suffering to be expected (Mark 10:38ff.); the Augsburg Confession refers to children as being surrendered (offered) to God,[69] the sacrificial response called for in faith;[70] and as a result of baptism the offering of good works.[71] The divine initiative demands a human response.

Confession and absolution is referred to as a third sacrament among Lutherans, a "genuine sacrament."[72] "It is taught among us that private absolution should be retained and not allowed to fall into disuse."[73] The emphasis is on the absolution rather than confession, and the reformers insist it should be encouraged rather than mandatory, and they did away with the concept of satisfaction as it has been understood by the late medieval church. "Confession is not abolished among us, for it is not usual to give the body of the Lord except to them that have been previously examined and absolved."[74] The emphasis in the Confessions is on the private nature of the confession, on the absolution that is pronounced, on the need to confess only those sins that one knows and feels in one's heart, on its frequency rather than being the exception, and it is "wicked" to abolish it.[75] It is clear that a large number of Lutherans today fall short of this ideal. Nor can it be said that pastoral counseling is a surrogate, for it is not synonymous with confession. *The Lutheran Book of Worship* includes a form, Individual Confession and Absolution (pp. 196–98), to encourage a revival of this salutary practice.

The human response to God's initiative includes the performance of good works as a result of faith, hearing God's Word and responding to it, living daily within the baptismal covenant, offering God thanks and praise in the Eucharist, and living in the awareness of the forgiveness of sins, the absolution offered by the church.

5

Divine Initiative:
Salvation in Orthodox Theology

What is the relationship between divine initiative and human initiative in the work of salvation?

To the Orthodox, who never knew the trauma and the resultant theological creativity of the Reformation, Western Christians seem to be polarized on this issue. While Roman Catholics hold that salvation depends on a substantial accumulation of merits through good works, Protestants (and especially Lutherans) reject works altogether as the products of a distorted "works-righteousness," in which God is bound by human initiative, and the cross of Christ is emptied of its saving power.

This is, of course, a simplistic view of both positions. But the fact that most Orthodox Christians hold to such caricatures illustrates a point worth remembering: that as outsiders we approach internecine disputes in Western Christendom from a different historical, cultural, and theological perspective. Especially in the so-called "diaspora"—outside of traditionally Orthodox lands—we have acquired something of a "bunker mentality" to preserve our faith and our worship from reductionist and relativizing tendencies so prevalent in the secularized popular religions of modern Western technocracies. Interfaith dialogue, however, is making increasingly clear the fact that every traditional Christian confession is threatened by these same tendencies. Through the grace and guidance of the Holy Spirit, ecumenical dialogue such as the one in which we are presently engaged will serve to break down our respective stereotypes and lead each of us back to the authentic sources of our Christian faith and life. By returning to these sources, many of which we hold in common, it may be possible for us to transcend our differences of history and culture, in order to discover the depth and breadth of the theology that does in fact unite us.

In his lucid and informative paper on "Human Participation in the Divine/Human Dialogue," Carl Volz has presented major issues of Lutheran theology in a way that should elicit significant agreement on the part of the Orthodox. Such issues include original sin and divine forgiveness, sacramental theology, Scripture, and liturgical worship. I would like to focus on some of these same issues in order to outline an Orthodox approach to the question of divine initiative in the work of salvation. This can be no more than a superficial and highly schematic overview. Its components will include the "immanent Trinity" (God in his innermost being), the "economic Trinity" (God in his relation to the created order), creation, anthropology, original sin, redemption, and finally *theōsis* or deification.

TRINITARIAN THEOLOGY

The Eastern church fathers begin and end their theological reflection with "revelation": self-disclosure of the divine life and purpose. God reveals himself in the natural order (Rom. 1:20), but only as the sovereign Creator, Lord, and Judge. Knowledge of God as Savior, who communicates to us the depths of his love and enables us to participate in his own divine life, is acquired by the special revelation that finds expression in Scripture, in the doctrinal affirmations of the ecumenical councils, and in the experience of the worshiping church. These complementary elements make up what we call holy tradition, which transmits knowledge of God for the salvation of humankind.

All revelation is ultimately soteriological. It is granted, as the eucharistic liturgy declares, "for the life of the world and its salvation." To the Greek fathers, however, this does not mean that we know God only in his acts or saving work. We also have knowledge, limited as it is, of God's inner life and being. Accordingly, they distinguish between *theologia* and *economia*, the former referring to relations within the godhead, and the latter to God's saving work within creation. True "theology," then, concerns what we may call the "immanent Trinity," whereas the work of salvation is an expression of the "economic Trinity," God *ad extra*. The distinction is somewhat artificial, but it is useful insofar as it enables us to affirm that our knowledge of God is not limited to his mighty acts within history but includes a perception or vision of God as he is within himself, apart from his relationship to creation. This revealed knowledge of God is most adequately expressed in the language of the first two ecumenical councils as the union of three divine persons (*hypostaseis*) in one divine nature or essence (*ousia*). According to the Cappadocian synthesis, the three hypostases are distinguished only in terms of their origin: the Father is eternally "unbegotten," the Son is eternally "begotten" of the Father, and the Spirit eternally "proceeds" from the Father. Consubstantial (*homoousios*) and without beginning, the three share not only a common nature but also a common will.

In human experience, the divine will is expressed as the "economy," the operation or action of God for the salvation of humanity and the cosmos as a whole. Utterly unknowable in his divine essence, God reveals himself and effects his will through the divine hypostases. Byzantine theology describes this "economy" in terms of a "pneumatic Christology." It stresses the absolute unity-without-confusion of the concerted operation of the Son and the Spirit in leading the faithful into knowledge of and communion with the Father.

Revelation and saving grace proceed from the Father, through the Son, and are manifested and made accessible by the Holy Spirit within the church. Pneumatic Christology discerns a double movement from the godhead toward the world. On the one hand, the faithful experience the presence of the saving power of the Word of God, and the Word or divine Son subsequently sends the Spirit upon the believing community. On the other hand, the Spirit sends the Son through the incarnation (Luke 1:35) and manifests him through the resurrection (1 Tim. 3:16); he then continues to reveal the Son or divine Word in the eschatological age of the church. This "double revelation"—of the Son by the Spirit and the Spirit by the Son—serves to communicate that unique knowledge of God that the Johannine Jesus equates with eternal life (John 17:3).

Salvation consists in "knowledge of God," acquired through revelation. Such knowledge, pertaining to both the "immanent" and the "economic" Trinity, depends wholly upon divine initiative. It is the Spirit who manifests the divine Word and inspires interpretation of the scriptural witness to that Word. It is the Spirit who makes that Word "the power of God for salvation to everyone who has faith" (Rom. 1:16).

The self-revelation that leads to knowledge of God and eternal communion with him is an expression of the common will and action of the three divine hypostases. It is a "personal" revelation that communicates divine life as an act of self-transcending love. While love unites the three persons within the godhead (the Spirit remaining a distinct hypostasis, and never reduced to a *nexus amoris*), in its inexhaustible depth and intensity that love overflows and surpasses the boundless limits of divine being in order to embrace, save, and transfigure the object of its affection.

CREATION

What is the object of God's saving love? To the Greek fathers it is not only humanity—men and women made in the image of God—but creation itself.

To Origen, creation is a function of the divine nature. Consequently, creation must be coeternal with that nature; hence Origen posits the eternity of the created order. Against this view, Saint Athanasius and the Orthodox consensus hold that creation is *ex nihilo*, being from non-being, accomplished as an expression of the divine will. God runs the awesome risk of positing a nature other than his own. Out of nothingness he "calls all things into being," so that creation has both an origin and a *telos*, a beginning and a fulfillment, when death shall be destroyed, and the Son shall subject himself and the cosmos as a whole (*ta panta*) to the Father, that "God might be all in all" (*panta en pasin*—1 Cor. 15:28).

This necessary and radical distinction between divine nature and created nature leads the fathers, from Athanasius to Gregory Palamas, to make a further distinction within the godhead. In order to express the mystery of divine intervention into the created order and still preserve the absolute otherness of God, they differentiate between the divine "essence" (*ousia*) and the divine "energies" or operations (*energeia*). While God remains wholly unknowable and inaccessible in his essence, he reveals himself and effects his will through his energies—his attributes such as love, mercy, wisdom, power, justice—that are often equated with divine grace. This is not, as has been charged, a gnosticizing theory of emanations. God is wholly present in the energies, drawing persons and the cosmos into communion with himself. Through the energies, he transfigures the cosmos. The initiative remains entirely his own; however, the objects of that initiative—humanity and the cosmos—are neither passive nor static. By virtue of created nature, humanity possesses an inner, dynamic capacity for response, one that engages the entire cosmos of which humanity is the microcosm. This God-given capacity—one of "freedom in responsibility"—makes it necessary for humans to engage in continuing repentance and in an ascetic struggle against demonic powers within the created order. But this capacity to respond in freedom to the divine initiative also offers people the possibility for self-transcending and transfiguring participation in the divine energies that lead to deification.

ANTHROPOLOGY

The human person is the most sublime expression of God's creative activity. Adam and Eve, man and woman, are created according to the image and likeness of God (Gen. 1:26). God is both the origin and the destiny of created human life. His "image" is realized in humanity not so much through particular attributes or capacities (love, reason, etc.) as through the distinctive personal quality that sets humans apart from and above every other created being, including the incorporeal beings of the angelic world. The image of God in people is identified by most Greek Orthodox theologians today (Yannaras, Zizioulas, Nissiotis, Nellas) with human "personhood": the divinely bestowed capacity for relationship with God, self, and others, exercised in freedom and love.

We are persons only insofar as we reflect the ultimate personhood of God. As persons, however, we are obliged to deal with what Yannaras calls "the existential adventure of [our] freedom." This is because the fall—understood both individually and collectively—forces us into a permanent situation of choice. The free decision to rebel against the divine will has placed humanity in a state of exile from paradise. Man or woman, according to Saint Basil, "is an animal who received the command to become God" [*Greg. Naz.* 43rd Oration]. By succumbing to temptation, however, people alienate themselves from God and betray their ultimate vocation. In Christ, we have the possibility of progressing "from one degree of glory to another" (2 Cor. 3:18), toward that full and perfect communion with divine life that provides the indispensable foundation for authentic humanity or personhood. The constant need to choose light and truth over darkness and deception, however, engages us in an ongoing inner struggle against demonic temptation and auto-idolatry. Genuine asceticism, then, is an indispensable element in the movement toward salvation. Consequently, the divine initiative must be met by human initiative, by

109

the exercise of human will—through repentance, prayer, and works of love—that enables humanity, created in the image of God, to assume, through a process of inner purification and sanctification, the *likeness* of God.

How do we understand "original sin" from this perspective? Orthodox theology is not as concerned as Lutheran theology with the tension between freedom and responsibility, free will and determinism. Nevertheless, we fully agree in our rejection of the scholastic dogma of original sin, particularly as it implies the transmission of the sin and guilt of Adam to succeeding generations, like some genetic defect. In fact, the Orthodox are loath to speak at all of original sin, unless we understand by that expression that the origin of one's sinfulness lies in oneself: in the corrupted, fallen will that retains the capacity for good yet freely (although inevitably at times) chooses evil. Romans 7 may depict "man [and woman] under the law," but it also says much about the struggle of the faithful Christian.

Both Lutheran and Orthodox teachings on original sin reflect a particular interpretation of Rom. 5:12 ("as sin came into the world through one man, and death came through sin, so death spread to all"). The crucial phrase is the one that follows: *eph' hō pantes hēmarton*. To what does the relative *eph' hō* refer? Western scholastic theology renders it "in whom," implying that all are subject to death because all sin "in Adam" (*in quo omnes peccaverunt*—Vulgate). In contrast, Eastern patristic tradition, followed by most Protestant versions (RSV, NRSV, NEB, etc.), render *eph' hō* as "because": all die "because" all commit sin. What is "inherited" from Adam, then, is not the stain of guilt in consequence of his sin in paradise. Rather, if we can speak of "inheritance" at all, it must be seen as the inheritance of *mortality*: "death spread to all 'because' all sin." Humanity has willfully corrupted any capacity for self-determination (*autexousia*); self-idolatry has alienated people from God and from communion with divine life. Mortality has come upon human life as a result of disobedience: mortality being understood as the natural consequence of a rupture in communion with the source of life, or as the divinely imposed limit placed upon human temporal existence so that alienation does not last forever. In this latter case, divine initiative takes the form of judgment upon sin as well as mercy toward sinners, imposing death as a means for ending human exile and eventually bringing people into communion with the source of eternal life.

Thus sin and death are seen as corrupting powers that are mutually causative. While death enters because of sin, death is also a source of sin. The rendering of *eph' hō* by "because" implies that death itself is the origin of sin. *Eph' hō*, according to this interpretation, refers to *thanatos*, and the phrase can be understood to mean that we commit sin "because of death." In other words, the motor behind sin is the desperate attempt to escape death and consequent meaninglessness.

Although sin and death are conceived, in Pauline fashion, as enslaving cosmic powers, they are limited in their capacity to corrupt and destroy humanity. Orthodox theology (with Carl Volz—and against both Calvin and Luther) has never held that sin has totally effaced the divine image in humans. Nor is the human will totally corrupted through disobedience. Humanity is created essentially "good," as is all of God's handiwork. While the divine image may be badly tarnished and all but obscured, a dimension of the human will—the "gnomic" as opposed to the "natural" will, according to Saint Maximos the Confessor—possesses a capacity for freedom of choice. Understood as a function of the human person rather than of being—a hypostatic rather than a natural property—the gnomic will can respond to the divine initiative in faith, love, and obedience. Repentance is an enduring possibility even in the blackest hearts. This is because sin originates with the "personal" rather than the natural dimension of human existence. It is through this personal aspect of one's life—the aspect that transcends nature and permits communion with God—that freedom operates to produce the fruits of repentance that open the way toward personal deification.

The human will is in bondage, as Luther—and modern psychology—affirm. But that bondage is relative and limited. Saint Maximos's distinction between the natural will (*thelēma physikon*) and the gnomic will (*thelēma gnōmikon*) is useful, insofar as it holds in proper tension both the bondage and the freedom of the human will. Thereby it deals realistically with the antinomy of determinism and free will, while resolving the problem of freedom and responsibility. It also safeguards human initiative as an indispensable element in the "divine-human dialogue." For Orthodox theology, therefore, salvation is accomplished only through "synergy": a cooperation between God and the person that culminates in the deification of the creature. Yet Orthodoxy, like Lutheranism, rejects the scholastic notion of "operating" and "cooperating" grace. Salvation and deification cannot be expressed by categories of cause and effect. Synergy implies a fundamental (and non-Pelagian) paradox: the initiative is wholly divine, originating and coming to completion within Trinitarian divine life; yet an appropriate human response is necessary for the appropriation of saving grace. This does not mean that God is active and the person is passive. *Askēsis* involves action, as do repentance, prayer, and works of love. The initiative, however, remains in the hands of God, together with the sanctifying grace that transforms bearers of the divine image "from one degree of glory to another." A person merely responds to that grace, by welcoming and interiorizing it in his or her personal existence.

To Saint Maximos, however, human initiative goes beyond a strictly personal response. It includes a cosmic aspect as well. Humanity is a microcosm, with the vocation to overcome the various divisions introduced into creation through the fall: divisions between uncreated and created being, the celestial and terrestrial, intelligible and sensible, paradise and the world of fallen natural phenomena, even between male and female. This awesome task is accomplished through the practice of specific virtues. Chastity overcomes sexual division, love overcomes cosmic division, etc., until, through personal initiative, a person exercises the priestly function of offering creation back to God. This process, by which the fundamental divisions are healed, results finally in the deification of humanity and the transfiguration of the cosmos. Once again, however, the initiative in the process belongs to God and to God alone. The virtues that permit those divisions to be overcome are bestowed by God in the form of deifying energies—energies that are actualized again in the experience of the church through the cosmic dimension of the eucharistic liturgy, which we call "divine."

REDEMPTION

The central dogma of Orthodox life and faith is that "the Word became flesh" (John 1:14). During the third and fourth centuries, Trinitarian theology was worked out on the basis of ecclesial reflection concerning the person of Jesus Christ. While the doctrine of the Trinity may be logically prior to every other, the center or wellspring from which all other doctrines flow remains the assumption of human nature by the eternal Logos. The touchstone of Orthodoxy, therefore, is its Christology.

Arian, Nestorian, and Monophysite heresies all managed to distort the scriptural witness to the person of the Son of God, by questioning either his full humanity or his full divinity. The Chalcedonian definition of 451 strove for balance. It recognized the diversity that exists among New Testament Christologies, and it tried to reconcile that diversity in a synthesis that reflected ecclesial experience. If Nicea I (A.D. 325) had proclaimed the Son *homoousios* with the Father, Chalcedon affirmed that through the incarnation he fully assumed our human nature, becoming like us in everything but sin (Heb. 4:15; 7:26; 1 Pet. 2:22; 1 John 3:5, etc.). In the one person of the Logos two natures, human and divine, are perfectly united "without confusion," "without change," "indivisibly" and "inseparably." Since will is a function of nature (rather than of person), the Sixth Ecumenical Council (Constantinople III, 680–681) affirmed "duotheletism": the presence of two wills in the incarnate Word. Thereby the humanity of Christ is preserved intact against any "monophysite" tendency to absorb humanity into divinity.

Yet the Chalcedonian definition, together with succeeding clarifications accepted as Orthodox, insists that the union of humanity and divinity in the incarnate Logos is "asymmetrical." That is, the person or subject who becomes incarnate remains the eternal, divine Son of God, for it is God alone—and not a human person—who can save us. Rather than diminish the assumed humanity, however, the incarnation renews and restores it to its original fullness and perfection. While remaining the eternal divine Word, the Son of God becomes the last Adam. Yet he is also the archetypal Adam. As the visible image of the invisible Father (Col. 1:15), who "is the exact imprint of God's very being [hypostasis]" (Heb. 1:3), he serves as the model or divine paradigm of personal human existence. Therefore, because he is consubstantial both with the Father and with humankind, he is able to mediate salvation and open the way to the hypostatic deification of the believer. In the words of the author of Hebrews, "He had to become like his brothers and sisters in every respect [except for sin, understood as a 'lack' rather than as a positive attribute], so that he might be a merciful and faithful high priest in the service of God, to make a sacrifice for the sins of the people" (2:17).

The late Father Georges Florovsky warned of a rebirth of ancient heresies in today's pluralistic world: neo-Arianism, neo-Nestorianism, etc. Most Orthodox would be glad if modern christological reflection produced nothing less reductionist than that.

Many believe they see the real danger lying in some hidden agenda devised by "liberal" Protestants and Catholics, whose "sinister" purpose is to undermine the faith, and salvation itself, by reducing Jesus Christ to an ordinary human being and denying his divinity altogether. Having read nothing other than popularized versions of the more radical views, they conclude that the "heterodox" as a block reject the traditional, conciliar formulations of Christology and Trinitarian theology and *ipso facto* undermine the Christian faith they profess. The non-Orthodox react with either amusement or frustration at their Orthodox counterparts, who cling to what they perceive to be a non-biblical, strictly metaphysical approach to a doctrinal question that would be better dealt with by using existential rather than ontological categories. Why in fact do the Orthodox continue to insist on the need for an ontological rather than an existential approach to the person of Jesus Christ and his saving work?

The answer, in the briefest terms, lies in the truths expressed by two patristic formulas. The first is the familiar affirmation, found in various forms in the early fathers, that we usually associate with Saint Athanasius: "God became man so that man might become god (or: divine)." This declares the fundamental Orthodox conviction that the human vocation, or ultimate *raison d'être*, is to become by grace what God is by nature. In other words, the end (*telos*) of human existence is "participation" (*koinōnia, methexis*) in divine life. This is the original vocation accorded to Adam, the vocation he and every person rejects by a free decision to rebel against the divine will. Adam is "fallen." Human nature is corrupted, subjected to the forces of death and decay. The bondage to sin and death consequently involves nature, not merely existential relationship. Fallen human nature must be restored to its original glory, a glory derived from its creation in the divine image. That fallen nature, however, cannot save itself from the powers of sin and death, nor can it accomplish the restoration of the divine image through its own efforts. Therefore people need a Redeemer who not only identifies with the human condition, but who also assumes, liberates, and exalts human nature with himself, through his own victory over the corrupting power of death.

The second formula, in the words of Saint Gregory of Nazianzus, expresses the necessity for the Creator to assume the fullness of created nature in order to restore that nature to its original meaning, wholeness, and beauty: "What is not assumed is not healed, but what is united to God is saved" [Ep. 101 *ad Cledonium*].

Alternative theologies of redemption focus upon the forensic category of justification or the expiatory character of vicarious sacrifice. Byzantine theology, of course, accepts the Pauline concept of *dikaiosunē* (understanding it more as divine "righteousness" than "justification") and other New Testament images that speak of the atoning value of Christ's sacrifice ("Lamb of God," "expiation," "ransom," etc.). Yet perhaps it is not too much of an exaggeration to say that the Greek fathers were more concerned with *who* died on the cross than with the question of why that form of death was necessary. Again, ontological—rather than forensic or sacrificial—categories are called into play. As a result, Orthodoxy expresses its entire understanding of Christ's redemptive death in a doctrine of *theopaschism:* in the words of Saint Cyril of Alexandria, "The Logos suffered in the flesh." That is, for God to save his human creatures, he had to assume—in the person of the divine Son—the fullness of human nature, then die and rise again in that nature, so that by his exaltation through the ascension he might glorify humanity with himself and lead humankind to a deifying participation in divine life.

"What is not assumed is not saved." That affirmation does not simply concern human nature in the abstract, for a "nature" must by "hypostatized." In the expression of Leontius of Byzantium, Christ "enhypostatizes" human life in his own divine hypostasis. Although the subject of the incarnation remains the eternal Son, he nevertheless assumes personal human existence, including the necessity of death. He who dies on the cross, and descends into the realm of death to raise the dead with himself, is none other than the God-man. While "patri-passionism" is rigorously excluded (the Son—not the Father—suffers and dies), "theopaschism" remains the irreducible foundation of any Orthodox theology of redemption.

If Orthodoxy makes little use of such theories as "justification," "satisfaction," and "vicarious atonement" to explain the way Christ accomplishes our salvation, it is for at least two reasons. First, such concepts seem to reflect the Roman Catholic-Protestant dispute over the way the guilt of original sin is removed: either by meritorious works, or by the free gift of God's grace (conceived as "forgiveness of sins" or as "imputed righteousness," as in Luther's *simul justus et peccator*). As we have seen, this question was not an issue in the development of the Orthodox doctrine of (original) sin. The second reason, and the most important, is that none of the traditionally Western theories of justification, atonement, etc., really necessitates personal divine involvement in the death that accomplishes our redemption. If many Western theologians tend to minimize the divinity of Christ today—or at least to neglect the conciliar formulations of Christology and Trinitarian theology—is it not due to the fact that Western theories of redemption and salvation simply do not require that Jesus Christ be ontologically identified with the godhead? The Chalcedonian definition must be defended as the cornerstone of Christian faith only if Jesus of Nazareth must have been "God in the flesh"—only if God had to assume humanity without change, die upon the cross, descend into hell and break the bonds of death by his resurrection, and ascend into glory "in the flesh" (Saint Ignatius)—in order to accomplish our salvation. Yet this is precisely what Orthodoxy affirms and why it has such difficulty with any other approach that seems to limit salvation to a matter of justification or atonement. To the Orthodox justification is merely the beginning of a process of eternal duration. Salvation is not the end or *telos* of human existence; it is merely the negative aspect that achieves liberation from the consequences of sin and death. The true meaning of God's work in Christ can only be seen in the ongoing process that leads from initial salvation, through sanctification, and on to a "deification by grace" of the human person.

THEŌSIS OR DEIFICATION

The ontological participation of God in the human condition opens the way for human participation in the being of God. If the *telos* of human existence were less than a total sharing in triune life— if people were called, for example, to mere "fellowship" with God through justification or even to eternal enjoyment of the "beatific vision"—then it would have been theoretically possible for God to work out salvation without resorting to a true incarnation that required the eternal divine Logos to accept death in his assumed humanity. Full ontological participation of God in our human life is necessary if we are to know the same quality and degree of participation in his divine life.

The significance of the cross of Christ is ultimately that of liberation: from death and corruption, from anxiety, and from sin. Of course each of these remains a reality in daily life, for the Christian as much as for the nonbeliever. The liberating power of the crucifixion concerns the ultimate victory over those experiences as it is so poignantly depicted in the eschatological imagery of the final chapters of Revelation, when God, dwelling in the midst of his people, "will wipe every tear from their eyes," and "Death will be no more" (21:4).

Nevertheless, the death of the Son of God within human history effects a liberating transformation of human life already within the scope of that history. This "existential freedom"—a freedom "in the Spirit"—is what enables us to respond to the divine initiative with faith and love. This freedom, then, serves as the indispensable ground of our sanctification.

Like salvation, sanctification is a process based upon synergy or divine-human cooperation. Here again the initiative belongs wholly to God. It is the Spirit who communicates truth, who bestows gifts, and who fills our hearts with the love of the Father within the body of Christ. It is the Spirit who elicits faith, confers grace, and inspires virtues that take the form of "works of love." Without our active receptivity, however, his work would come to nothing. In other words, if the work of sanctification is to proceed, divine initiative must be met by a moral response on our part.

Carl Volz expresses this same idea when he affirms that "justification makes the sinner 'good' . . . There is an ontological change in Baptism that brings with it the indwelling Christ and the very real presence of the Holy Spirit" (p. 97). This indicates that we as Orthodox must broaden our understanding of justification and link it vitally to the process of sanctification, as Lutheran theology seems to do. If this linkage is made from both of our perspectives, then the gulf that has separated those who profess "justification by faith alone" from those who insist on synergy and ascetic purification may yet prove to be an illusion created more by language than by actual behavior. Both Lutherans and Orthodox insist that faith must issue in love, while both agree that such works of love are merely our ethical response to grace and not the grounds of our salvation.

Carl Volz also points out important affinities that exist between the Lutheran teaching on sanctification and the Orthodox doctrine of deification. What separates the two is not so much a matter of substance as degree: the Orthodox holding that "divinization" or "deification" means a literal, "ontological" participation in the being of God. To avoid any hint of absorption into the divinity with a consequent loss of individual personality, Byzantine theology bases its teaching about deification on two complementary themes. First, it holds that in Christ the true humanity, including the unique personal identity, of each human being is preserved and restored to its original fullness and beauty. Second, taking up the distinction between essence and energies that goes back at least to Saint Gregory of Nyssa, the Greek patristic tradition affirms that deification is achieved by grace, through the sanctifying power of the divine energies. Humans are not, nor can we ever be "participants of the divine nature," if by nature we understand not "being" (as 2 Pet. 1:4) but the divine essence. For the latter is transcendent and inaccessible to any form of created reality. "Deification," therefore, does not suggest that we become God, despite the rather audacious language used by some of the early patristic writers. It means that by the initiative that belongs wholly to the three Divine Persons, humans as creatures are introduced into personal relationships of participation in the uncreated, divine energies or grace. Thereby people become "by grace" what God is "by nature."

In the context of this dialogue it would perhaps be appropriate to conclude by indicating how Byzantine theology grounds its understanding of *theōsis* in Scripture.

Plato spoke of a transformation of human life through *anamnēsis* that issues in a certain likeness of God, and Gnosticism taught divinization as the fruit of *gnōsis*. Hebrew thought knows nothing of such language, nor of the dualistic ideas behind it, largely because of its instinctive concern to preserve divine transcendence and avoid any confusion between the created and the uncreated. It is clear that the early Christian patristic writers employed verbs such as *theopoiein*, and later the noun *theōsis*, to describe the end of human existence. Did they merely adopt and attempt to Christianize language and ideas of purely Hellenistic provenance? Or does their language reflect concepts that are authentically biblical? Just how faithful to the apostolic witness are expressions such as *genētai Theos* (Theophilus of Antioch, *ad Autolycum* 2:27) or even the assertions of Saint Ignatius of Antioch that we are "god-bearers" (*theophoroi*), called to be "partakers of God" (*Theou metexēte—ad Eph.* 9:2; 4:2; cf. *Poly.* 6:1)?

Without going into an exegesis of the texts, we can point to a significant variety of New Testament passages that serve to ground—and to authenticate—the patristic teaching on deification.

The classic passage is 2 Peter 1:4, which affirms that through God's great promises "you may escape from the corruption that is in the world because of lust, and may become participants of the divine nature" (*genēsthe theias koinōnoi physeōs*). This verse is not without difficulties, as we have seen, because it affirms what Orthodoxy adamantly rejects—that our participation is in the very nature of God. Of course language was fluid in the early second century when this writing was produced. (We may recall that even in the fourth century Saint Cyril of Alexandria could speak of "one nature [*physis*] of God incarnate.")

More solid ground is provided by several New Testament writers, from Saint Paul and Saint John to the author of Hebrews. Paul's teaching on filial adoption (Gal. 3:26; 4:5; cf. Acts 17:28), for example, together with his blessing that invokes the *koinōnia* of the Spirit (2 Cor. 13:13), lead clearly in the direction of participation in divine life. Still more significant are his expressions that issue from his so-called "Christ mysticism": expressions such as *en* and *syn Christō*, and the exclamation, "It is no longer I who live, but it is Christ who lives in me" (Gal. 2:20). Both Paul and John speak (in accordance with teachings of late Judaism) of a transfiguring and assimilating "vision" of God, when at the Parousia we shall behold Christ and ourselves in our true glory: "When he is revealed, we will be like him" (*homoioi autō*—1 John 3:2; cf. 1 Cor. 13:12).

The clearest basis for a doctrine of *theōsis* in the Johannine writings is found in the concept of mutual indwelling expressed by the verb *menein*. As the Spirit descends upon Christ at his baptism and indwells him (John 1:32), so that same Spirit indwells the believer (John 14:17; 1 John 3:24; 4:13). The Johannine concept of "eternal life," accessible already within earthly human existence and brought to fulfillment at the eschaton (John 5:21-29), likewise attests to the authentic participation of human in divine existence.

Another key concept is that of "partaking" or participation, expressed by the verb *metechō* and its cognates, or by the phrases *(syn)koinonos ginomai*. Saint Paul accepts his apostolic mission in order that he might partake of the blessings of the gospel (1 Cor. 9:23), called in Colossians "the inheritance of the saints in the light . . . into the kingdom of his [God's] beloved Son" (1:12-13). The author of Hebrews takes this a step further when he speaks of our share in or partaking of "a heavenly calling" (3:1), and he declares that we are made partakers of Christ (3:14) and of the Holy Spirit (6:4). Finally, the apostle Paul again affirms that those who rise in Christ will "put on" God's own incorruptible immortality (1 Cor. 15:52-57; cf. 2 Cor. 4:16–5:8).

Many other passages could be cited, all of which seem to reflect two things: Jesus' own teaching on believers' participation in the kingdom, manifested in his person; and the living experience of the church, in which the Pauline Christ-mysticism becomes a personal, transfiguring reality. To be "in Christ," through baptismal grace to which we respond in faithfulness and love, is already a foretaste of the coming, total participation in divine life. Like "eternal life" in the perspective of Saint John, deification is a present possibility for those who dwell in Christ and the Spirit.

We have no illusions that those who reject the notion of deification would agree that these passages admit this interpretation and no other. A certain extrapolation is needed to move from the New Testament to the patristic teaching on *theōsis*, just as it is to move from the biblical image of God dwelling in "unapproachable light" (1 Tim. 6:16) to the Athonite *hesychast* experience in which that light is beheld by the eyes of the flesh. This kind of extrapolation can only be made legitimately on the basis of ecclesial experience, where the living Word of God is actualized through liturgical celebration and sacramental grace.

Lutherans and Orthodox alike share in that experience. For our dialogue to move ahead, it would seem appropriate to look more closely at the common experience of faith, grace, and sanctification that is ours through worship. Equally important, however, is the attempt to reach a consensus on the "ontological" question raised in connection with both Christology and deification. Is it possible to reaffirm together the traditional apostolic and patristic conception of Jesus as "one" with the Father, in essence as well as in will, in order to give meaning to our respective teachings on salvation? In any event, whether we prefer the term "sanctification" or "deification," it is of vital importance to affirm that the ultimate meaning and goal of human existence is not only "to love God and to enjoy him forever," but to share fully in the glory of his divine life.

6

The Image of God in Classical Lutheran Theology

The *imago dei*, like certain other teachings that mark the churches of the Augsburg Confession, was forged within the matrix of Western theology. Nurtured in the theological traditions of late medieval scholasticism, the reformers inherited patterns of thinking and language that not only set the agenda but also the tone of theological discussion. However, they found the conventional understanding of the image of God to be imperfect and deficient when measured against the gospel. Their criticism of received ideas spawned a fresh set of considerations that allowed them to retrieve aspects of biblical and patristic tradition that had been overshadowed by the philosophical preoccupations of scholasticism. As a consequence the image of God came to function more as a soteriological and christological category than as an anthropological idea. Their approach, however, did have the consequence of restricting the theological utility of the image of God, and in time it came to play a much less significant role in Lutheran thinking than it had in earlier Christian thought.

BRIEF OVERVIEW OF EARLY BELIEFS

Medieval theology distinguished between the image and similitude of God. The image was understood to refer to the condition of being human, to those things that set human beings apart from animals, e.g., intellect, freedom of the will, et al., the similitude to a relation with God, to fellowship with God, what had come to be called *justitia originalis* (Peter Lombard, Sent. 2, dist. 16, a. 4). This original righteousness was understood to have been added to the image (hence the phrase *donum superadditum*), and was seen as a gift of grace. In this scheme, after the fall the similitude was lost but the image remained.

Saint Thomas Aquinas explained the distinction between image and similitude. He asked: "Utrum similitudo ab imagine convenienter distinguatur." (Should similitude properly be distinguished from image?) (*Prima Pars.* q. 93, art. 9). His answer was that they should be distinguished because similitude is "subsequent to image" and "signifies a certain perfection of image" (*aliquam perfectionem ipsius*). In support of this view he cited Saint Augustine who, like others, had observed that the two terms are not mentioned "without reason." If they had the same meaning one term would have been sufficient (*divers. quaest.*, 51). Saint Thomas also cited John of Damascus (*fid. orth.* 2.12) who said that image referred to mental capacity and free will, whereas likeness referred to virtue. Similitude was understood by medieval Western theologians to refer to something beyond the image, to a completing or perfecting of the image. This was the tradition in which Martin Luther and other reformers had been educated. In his commentary on Genesis Luther wrote: "They [the scholastics] say that the similitude lies in the gifts of grace. Just as similitude is a certain perfection of an image, so they say, our nature is perfected through grace."[1]

In the history of Christian thought the distinction between image and likeness goes back to Saint Irenaeus. He understood image to refer to reason and freedom of the will and likeness to signify the endowment of the Spirit (*haer.* 5.6.1; 3.23.5). The LXX had rendered the two Hebrew terms as *eikon* and *homoiosis*, respectively (Lat. *imago* and *similitudo*). In Greek, *eikon* was the normal term for image or copy and this implied that the *eikon* was inferior to the original or its exemplar. *Homoiosis* meant resemblance or likeness (its opposite was *alloiosis*), but it came to mean communion or assimilation with the exemplar. *Homoiosis* was used in an explicitly theological sense as early as Plato to speak of "likeness to God." The human being was said to be a being "like God" (Theatetus 176a). Likeness to God, however, was something to be achieved. The person who was willing and eager to be righteous, writes Plato, will never be neglected by God, and "by practicing virtue he will become like God (ὁμοιόεσθαι θεῷ) insofar as that is possible for a human being" (Rep. 613a). *Homoiosis* designated a goal, the end toward which one strived, the *telos* of human life.

In the early church, however, the distinction between image and similitude was not maintained rigorously.[2] The terms were often used interchangeably to speak of the creation of the human being according to a divine "model." Thus Saint Gregory of Nyssa made no distinction between image and likeness in his *On the Making of Man* and his *Great Catechism.* "The human being was created in the image of the divine nature, and along with other blessings he retains this divine likeness by having free will." (*or. cat. mag.* 21; see also *op.* 5 and 16).

The fathers, however, were consistent in affirming that image or likeness of God referred to the uniquely human characteristics of human beings, notably free will and rationality.

> There is in us the possibility for everything good, for all virtue and wisdom, and every better thing that can be conceived; but one thing is preeminent among all, that we are free from necessity, and are not subject to any natural power, but have within ourselves the power to choose what we wish. Virtue is self-determined and voluntary, for that which is subject to compulsion and coercion cannot be virtue (*de opificio hominis* 16.11).

The reasoning here is that human beings are moral creatures and virtue would have no meaning if they were not free, for actions undertaken as a result of coercion or necessity cannot be virtuous. This is an old, and one might add, sound argument that predates Christianity. It was adopted and elaborated by Christian thinkers already in the second century in answer to the charge (based on the biblical portrait of divine action) that the Christian (and Jewish) God was capricious and arbitrary and that human actions were determined by divine power and will. The story of the hardening of pharaoh's heart was often cited in this connection.

For the fathers, however, the doctrine of image of God was not simply a way of speaking about freedom of the will or rationality. They also recognized that image was used in the New Testament to designate that which had been lost in Adam and regained in Christ. In this context, i.e., in speaking of the restoration in Christ, the image was not conceived of as a permanent possession. Saint Basil of Caesarea writes:

> Human beings were created according to the image and likeness of God, but sin deformed (ἠχρείωσεν) the beauty of the image, drawing the soul to passionate desires. But God, who

made human beings, is the true life. Whoever has lost (ἀπο-λέσας) the likeness to God, lost fellowship with the light; whatever is without God is not able to share in the blessed light. Let us therefore return to the grace which we possessed from the beginning to which we have become strangers through sin. Let us again adorn ourselves according to the image of God, and through overcoming our passion become like the creator. For whoever in himself imitates the impassibility of the divine nature, insofar as it is possible, he will restore the image of God in his own soul (*sermo asceticus*, Garnier, 318d). [Note that image and likeness are used interchangeably.]

In this passage Saint Basil did not mention Christ, but it is evident that the concept of redemption as a restoration of the image is drawn from the Pauline texts that speak of Christ as the image of God. His older contemporary Saint Athanasius wrote:

What, then, was God to do? Or what was to be done save the renewing of that which was in God's image, so that by it human beings might come to more be able to know him? But how could this have come to pass save by the presence of the image of God itself, our Lord Jesus Christ. For by human means it was impossible, since they are but made after an image; nor by angels either, for not even they are [God's] images. Whence the Word of God came in his own person, that as he was the image of the Father, he might be able to create afresh the human being after the image . . . (de incarnatione 13).

When the image of God is used in this sense it is proper to say that the image was lost in the fall, as Saint Irenaeus wrote much earlier:

But when the [son of God] was incarnate and became man, he recapitulated in himself the long history of humankind and in a brief space of time he procured salvation for us, that what had been lost in Adam, i.e. being in the image and likeness of God, we obtain again in Christ Jesus (*adversus haereses* 3.18.1).

LUTHER'S VIEW OF THE IMAGE OF GOD

The reformers found the distinction between image and likeness gratuitous and contrived, a view that was derived from their reading of the Scriptures (the account in Genesis as well as Saint Paul), but which had been anticipated by patristic thought. Second, they thought the philosophical view of the image exaggerated human capability, and obscured the distinctively christological features of the image of God, thereby buttressing the role of works in salvation.

Martin Luther discussed the *imago dei* in his *Lectures on Genesis* delivered in Latin at the University of Wittenberg in 1535–1536.[3] The present text of Luther's commentary has been extensively reworked by its early editors and may not reflect Luther's own thinking on all points. But since our subject is not the "historical Luther" but the Lutheran theological tradition, the work can serve as a starting point for our discussion.

The topic of the image of God arises, as one would expect, when Luther reaches Gen. 1:26, "Let us make humankind in our image, according to our likeness." The first part of the verse prompts Luther to give a little disquisition on Trinitarian theology (because the image is an image of the Holy Trinity not God the Father) and then he takes up the distinction between "image and likeness." He first notes that Saint Augustine identified image with the powers of the soul: memory, mind (or intellect), and will. In this view, similitude lies in the gifts of grace, i.e., an intellect enlightened by faith, memory made confident through hope, and will adorned with love. Luther had no objection to using this Trinitarian scheme to interpret the image of God. What disturbed him was not a Trinitarian understanding of the image, but the conclusions drawn about free will.

> Therefore although I do not condemn or find fault with that effort and those thoughts by which everything is brought into relationship with the Trinity, I am not at all sure that they are very useful, especially when they are subsequently spun out further; for there is also added a discussion concerning free will, which has its origin in that image. This is what they maintain; God is free; therefore since man is created according to the image of God, he also has a free memory, mind and will.

Luther did not reject the traditional doctrine outright. He understood the reasoning that lay behind it. Characteristically, however, he said that he did not find it very useful—it did little to contribute to the life of faith. His theology almost always emerged out of his sensitivity as a pastor. The conventional formulation of the image of God failed to grasp the true nature of sin, hence it detracted from the magnitude of God's grace, and diminished Christ's role in redemption.

It must be remembered that in Luther's vocabulary free will had quite different overtones than it did in patristic thought. In antiquity it designated human responsibility for moral action. For Luther, however, free will excited considerable aversion because it signified the role of human effort in salvation; it was a code word to designate the exaltation of works over grace.

In his effort to place God's grace at the center of the Christian life, Luther edged away from the medieval teaching on the image of God. The image of God placed the accent at the wrong place, namely on human capability. He did not, however, abandon the image entirely and was willing to say that it remained after the fall. Yet, and this point is the most controversial: according to Luther the marks of the image, memory, will, and mind "are most depraved and most seriously weakened, yes, to put it more clearly, they are utterly leprous and unclean." On this basis the generation of Lutherans following Luther drew the necessary corollary: the image of God was not simply defaced or tarnished in the fall, it was lost.

Although Luther's criticism of the image of God had the result of displacing it from one area of theology, it had the positive effect of rehabilitating it elsewhere. The image of God, Luther argued, must be understood as something far greater than human will or intellect. Adam was a unique and perfect human being: "His inner and outer sensations were all of the purest kind. His intellect was the clearest, his memory was the best, and his will was the most straightforward—all in the most beautiful tranquility of mind without any fear of death and without any anxiety." The image of God signified that Adam knew God and believed, that he lived a holy and pure life, and that he trusted God fully and delighted in God's favor. For Luther, Adam was not an ordinary human being, not simply a man endowed with reason and will; he was the image of Christ and of redeemed humanity, a man for whom it was as natural to love God as it is for the eye to delight in light.

Once Adam fell into sin he no longer was the man God intended him to be. If we look at human history to find evidence of the image of God, said Luther, we will be disappointed. Few evidences of the image are to be found. "Not only have we had no experience of it, but we continually experience the opposite." The only place where one can actually see the image of God is to look at Christ, for only in him is there a "restoration of that image." Yet this is essential in understanding Luther's reasoning: even after putting on Christ human beings do not enjoy an untarnished image.

The image of God points to the eschaton, to the final fulfillment when God will bring all things to perfection. Only when we have been made perfect in Christ in the kingdom will we fully bear the impress of God's image. Then, says Luther, the will will be truly free, the mind truly enlightened, the memory persistent, and all other creatures will be under our rule "to a greater degree than they were in Adam's paradise." The redemption in Christ is not a return to a previous state, but the beginning of a new creation that is more glorious than the first creation.

OTHER INTERPRETATIONS AND CONCLUSIONS

With Luther's observations on Gen. 1:26 before us we can proceed to a brief consideration of several other classical texts within the Lutheran tradition. The earliest discussion of the image of God in Lutheran confessional writings is in the Apology to the Augsburg Confession. The topic there is original sin, and as in Luther's commentary on Genesis, behind the discussion lurks the medieval distinction between image and similitude. In the view of Philipp Melanchthon, the author of the Apology, the life of faith had been quantified and atomized, broken down into discrete acts of transgression and penance, thereby obscuring the biblical truth that sin in its most profound sense was not disconnected misdeeds but a turning away from God. In Melanchthon's provocative formulation, his opponents were troubled only by infractions against the second table of the Decalogue while they overlook offenses against the first table, "the more serious faults of human nature, namely ignoring God, despising him, lacking fear and trust in him . . ."[4]

The specific target of Melanchthon's criticism is the distinction between image and similitude and the notion of "original righteousness." He wishes to argue that *justitia originalis* is not something added to the first human being, as though, in the words of Luther, it was like a garland placed on the head of a beautiful maiden. Righteousness belongs to the image itself, and when the Scriptures say that man was created in the image of God and after his likeness it means that Adam feared and trusted in God. In support, he first cites Saint Irenaeus and then Saint Ambrose who wrote: "That soul is not in the image of God in which God is not always present." Further, he mentions Col. 3:10 (and Eph. 5:9) where Saint Paul speaks of putting on a new self "which is being renewed in knowledge according to the image of its creator." The image of God, then, is defined by what is regained in Christ. Hence it does not signify the condition of being human, but the actual relation with God expressed in faith and love. In Luther's words: "The likeness and image of God consists in the true and perfect knowledge of God, supreme delight in God, eternal life, eternal righteousness, eternal freedom from care."[5]

In its formative period Lutheran theology collapsed the distinction between image and likeness, interpreting the image through the likeness (as understood in medieval theology), and identifying original righteousness with the image restored in Christ. Three considerations were important in leading to this interpretation. First, the distinction between image and similitude was deemed artificial and unnecessary (and without foundation in the New Testament). It detached the second table of the Decalogue from the first and distorted the character of righteousness. Righteousness, according to the Lutheran reformers, was knowledge, fear, trust, and love of God. Second, the distinction underestimates the gravity of sin. After the fall, human nature cannot believe in and love God without "certain gifts and help of grace," i.e., without the gift of the Holy Spirit. In Luther's words explaining the Third Article of the Apostles' Creed:

> I believe that by my own reason or strength I cannot believe in Jesus Christ, my Lord, or come to him. But the Holy Spirit has called me through the Gospel, enlightened me with his gifts, and sanctified and preserved me in true faith, just as he calls, gathers, enlightens, and sanctifies the whole Christian church on earth and preserves it in union with Jesus Christ in the one true faith.

After the fall we no longer had the capacity to love and trust God on our own. Finally, the image of God is to be understood primarily by reference to Christ and secondarily by reference to Adam.

In the seventeenth century, Lutheran dogmaticians set down arguments from Scripture, tradition, and reason in greater detail to defend and expound the line of thinking advanced in the early decades of the Reformation. They found support not only in Saint Paul, but also in Genesis and in the church fathers. John Gerhard, the greatest of the Lutheran teachers in this period, was the author of a Patrology, the first work by that title in Christian history, and his theological discussions were always supported by extensive citations from patristic and medieval writers.[6] In his section on the image of God he cites Gregory of Nyssa, Basil of Caesarea, John Chrysostom, Epiphanius, Theodoret of Cyrus, Tertullian, Ambrose, Augustine, John of Damascus, Bernard of Clairvaux, among others. On the specific point whether one should distinguish between image and similitude, Gerhard observes that although both "image" and "similitude" are used in Gen. 1:26, in the verse immediately following only image is used. Similitude is omitted. "So God created humankind in his own image, in the image of God he created them. . . ." Since the meaning of "let us make" is to be found in the actual execution of God's will, i.e., in the words that follow, "God created humankind in his own image," the statement of the execution of his will interprets the statement of intention. Hence the two terms image and similitude express the same thing. Similitude is to be understood (ἐξηγητικῶς), i.e., as an interpretation of imago. (Loci Theologici 9.1.18) (Gerhard also cites Gen. 5:3, Adam begot Seth "in his own image and likeness" where there is no distinction between image and likeness.)

A more important consideration for John Gerhard, however, was Col. 3:9-10; there Paul speaks of redemption as a recovery of the image of God. "Do not lie to one another, seeing that you have stripped off the old self with its practices and have clothed yourselves with the new self, which is being renewed in knowledge according to the image of its creator." Similarly in Eph. 4:24, again speaking of redemption, Paul says that in Christ we put on a "new self, created according to the likeness of God in true righteousness and holiness." If the image is restored and regained in Christ, argues John Gerhard, it must have been lost in the fall.

> The apostle teaches that the new man is renewed in knowledge according to the image of him who created him. . . . Therefore the image of God is not found in human beings unless they are renewed by the Holy Spirit; for that which is acquired through renewal, is not present in the old man; for the gift obtained through regeneration can not be possessed through human generation.

By starting with soteriology, not anthropology, Lutheran theologians arrived at the conclusion that the medieval distinction between image and similitude, useful as it was for other purposes, blurred the central theological claims of the gospel. Nevertheless, once the controversies of the sixteenth century had passed and

Lutheran thinkers began to work out the consequences of the theological (and polemical) positions taken in the heat of dispute, they recognized that it was not sufficient to define the image of God solely in soteriological terms. Again John Gerhard was representative of the tradition. At the end of a long discussion of the image of God he posed the following question: "An imago Dei in homine per lapsum sit amissa?" (Has the image of God been lost in the fall?) He replied with four arguments (he stated them as conditions) supporting the position that it had not been lost and one argument to defend the view that it had been lost. All depend on the definition of image of God.

1. If the image is understood to be the essence of the soul, intellect, will, and other capabilities it is not lost through the fall.

2. If the image of God is understood to be a kind of general congruence between the soul of human beings and God, i.e., a kind of rational faculty, it is not lost through the fall.

3. If the image of God is understood to mean dominion over other living creatures, then the image is not lost through the fall.

4. If the image of God means certain principles born in us, faint traces in the mind and will, then the image is not lost through the fall.

5. But if the image of God is understood to mean "righteousness and true holiness" then the image of God has been lost in the fall.

The first four statements recapitulate medieval teaching on the image of God and recognize the necessity for Christian theology to offer a cogent philosophical doctrine of man. For this purpose the image of God is the most readily available theological category. Image of God is a biblical term that has come to designate the characteristic features of human beings before and after the fall, before grace and after grace.

Human beings possess free will, intellect, speech, memory and are the only living creatures to have history and culture. The image of God sets human beings apart from animals. This image was not lost in the fall; human history and culture are evidence of this image. If the distinctive marks of humanity were lost in the fall, it would follow that what came into being *post lapsum* was a different kind of creature, a teaching all Christian theology finds abhorrent. The Jesuit theologian and polemicist Robert Bellarmine tried to pin this charge on Lutheranism (resurrecting the Manichaean heresy) and John Gerhard rejected it by stating that it would be a very great heresy if the image of God was understood to designate the "essence of the soul" and the essence of human beings was said to have been lost in the fall. If this were so human beings would have lost their distinctive character, that which makes them human, and a new soul subject to sin would have been created. This soul, he continued, would be the work of the devil and incapable of redemption.

In conclusion, the image of God continued to serve Lutheran theology as a way of speaking about the uniqueness and excellence of the human being as created by God. In this way the Lutheran tradition stands within the broad stream of patristic and medieval tradition that saw freedom of the will, reason, human responsibility, capacity for virtue, dominion over the earth as marks of the divine image. This image was not lost, but only tarnished in the fall.

Yet the "anthropological" view of the image of God, i.e., image as a philosophical category that designates the unique features of the human animal, was not the central concern of the Lutheran theologians, at least during the Reformation in its formative period, nor for most of Lutheran history.[7] The Lutheran dogmaticians of the seventeenth century were comprehensive and balanced thinkers, men who weighed arguments carefully and sought to eliminate logical contradictions in their systems of theology. They were as respectful of human reason, philosophy, and the sciences as they were of Scripture and tradition. In this respect their intellectual work resembled that of the medieval scholastic theologians. They were, however, exponents of a tradition of Christian piety and thinking that took a fresh look at inherited teaching and practice. Certain convictions about sin, grace, and faith formed their outlook. It was these convictions, first stated with ardor and passion in Luther's exegesis of the Scriptures, and later formulated, often sharply, in the Lutheran Confessions,[8] that shaped and molded their theological systems. Like a stone thrown into a river whose ripples flow downstream, the eruption of the sixteenth century continued to reverberate even as the tradition was given systematic formulation.

Behind any discussion of the image of God lay the teaching on sin and redemption in Christ. John Gerhard wrote: "Proinde negare, quod amissa sit imago Dei, est ipsum peccatum originale negare." (Moreover to deny that the image of God has been lost is to deny original sin itself) (9.9.130). He has reference to Paul's words that before the coming of Christ we were in darkness (Eph. 5:8), that we cannot submit to God's law (Rom. 8:7), that before Christ we were "dead through trespasses and sins" and "by nature children of wrath" (Eph. 2:1, 3). His argument was that the very fact of redemption, the renewal of the Holy Spirit, is proof that the Holy Spirit had been lost, which is to say that the image had been lost. As a result of the fall we "turned against (*aversi*) God" and those who were once righteous became unrighteous, those who were healthy are sick, those once free are slaves, or in more flamboyant language, those who once bore the "beautiful image of God have been clothed with the dark mask of the devil" (9.9.130–132).

Lutherans believe that this view of the image of God, because of its christological orientation, is more faithful to the biblical tradition. The image is not defined according to human rational faculties or capabilities, nor according to the differences between human beings and animals, i.e., in relation to nature, but in relation to God and the revelation in Christ. By speaking of the image as effaced or lost, rather than simply tarnished or defaced, Lutherans stress the reality of sin in human life, that human beings, even with rationality and free will, nevertheless turn against God and his ways. Such a view of the image also makes place for the teleological or eschatological dimension of Christian faith. What is gained in Christ is greater than what was lost in Adam. In the language of the Exultet in the Easter liturgy: "O happy fault that was worthy to have so great a Redeemer." Or in the words of John Gerhard:

> By the grace of Christ and the power of the Holy Spirit, that image of God into which we have begun to be remade in this life, will one day shine in us more brightly and more gloriously than it once shone in Adam, for he was *able not* to die, but we are *not able* to die [ille poterat non mori, nos non poterimus mori] (9.10.138).

7

Election:
A Lutheran-Biblical View

DEFINITIONS FROM CONSERVATIVE LUTHERAN AUTHORS

"Election is the ordaining of God unto salvation."[1] Predestination or election denotes:

> all that God does in time for our conversion, justification and final glorification is based on, and flows from, an eternal decree of election or predestination, according to which God before the foundation of the world chose us in His Son Jesus Christ out of the mass of sinful mankind unto faith, the adoption of sons, and everlasting life.[2]

The decree of predestination is:

1. An eternal act of God (Eph. 1:4; 2 Thess. 2:13; 2 Tim. 1:9)
2. Who for His Goodness sake (2 Tim. 1:9; Rom. 9:11; 11:15)
3. Because of the merit of the foreordained Redeemer of all mankind (2 Tim. 1:9; Eph. 1:4; 3:11)
4. Purposed to lead into everlasting life (Acts 13:48; 2 Tim. 1:9; 2:10; Rom. 8:28, 29)
5. By way and means of salvation designated for all mankind (Rom. 8:28, 29; Eph. 1:4; 1 Peter 1:2)
6. A certain number (Acts 13:48; Matt. 20:16; 22:14)
7. Of certain persons (2 Tim. 2:19; 1 Peter 1:2; John 13:18)
8. And to procure, work and promote what would pertain to their final salvation (Rom. 8:30; Eph. 1:11; 3:10, 11; Mark 13:20-22).[3]

"Election is the eternal act of God with respect to all who are saved, by which, out of pure grace and for Christ's sake, He purposed to endow them in time with the spiritual blessings of conversion, justification, sanctification, and preservation unto eternal life."[4]

THE BIBLICAL WITNESS[5]

The main Old Testament word that describes God's electing action is the verb *bahar,* connoting the idea of selecting a person or object after having carefully weighed the alternatives. We note the word used to describe David's choice of slingstones in his conflict with Goliath, 1 Sam. 17:40; the sons of God choosing wives, Gen. 6:2; Joshua's determination to serve God rather than idols, Josh. 24:22; Moses' challenge to the people to choose life rather than death, Deut. 30:19ff. The word suggests a preference for or a pleasure in the object chosen. In the Septuagint and the New Testament the corresponding verb is *eklegomai. Eklego* is commonly active in classical Greek, but the biblical writers always use it in the middle voice, with reflexive overtones: it thus means "choose out for oneself." *Haireomai* is used synonymously of God's choice in 2 Thess. 2:13, as in Deut. 26:18LXX. The cognate adjectives are *bahir* in Hebrew and *eklectos* in the Greek, consistently translated "elect" or "chosen." The New Testament also uses the noun *ekloge,* "election." The Hebrew verb *yada,* "know," which is used of various acts of knowing that, in idea at least, imply and express affections (e.g., relations between the sexes, and the believer's acknowledgment of God), is used to denote God's election (i.e., his taking cognizance of persons—in love) in Gen. 18:19 (RSV); Amos 3:2; Hos. 13:5. The Greek *prognosko,* "foreknow" is similarly used in Rom. 8:29; 11:2, to mean "forelove" (compare also the use of *ginosko* in 1 Cor. 8:3 and Gal. 4:9).

The Old Testament Expression

The faith of Israel was founded on the belief that she was God's chosen nation. His choice of her had been made by means of two connected and complementary acts: (1) He chose Abraham, by taking him out of Ur and bringing him to the promised land of Canaan making there an everlasting covenant with him, promising that his seed should be a blessing to all the earth. (Gen. 11:31—12:7; 15; 17; 22:15-18: Neh. 9:7; Isa. 41:8). (2) He chose Abraham's seed by redeeming them from slavery in Egypt, bringing them out of bondage under Moses, renewing the Abrahamic covenant with them in an amplified form at Sinai and setting them in the promised land as their national home (Exod. 3:6-10); Deut. 6:21-23; Ps. 105). Each of these acts of choice is also described as God's call, a sovereign utterance of words and disposal of events by which God summoned, in the one case, Abraham, and in the other, Abraham's seed to acknowledge him as their God and live to him as his people (Isa. 51:2; Hos. 11:1). Israelite faith looked back to these two acts as having created the nation (Isa. 43:1; Acts 13:17).

The meaning of Israel's election is drawn from the following facts: (1) Its source was God's free omnipotent love (Deut. 7:8; 23:5). (2) The goal of Israel's election was proximately, the blessing and salvation of the people through God's separating them for himself (Ps. 33:12), and ultimately, God's own glory through Israel's showing forth of his praise to the world (Isa. 43:20f.), and bearing witness to the great things he had done (Isa. 43:10-12; 44:8). (3) The religious and ethical obligations created by Israel's election were far reaching. Election, and the covenant relationship based on it, which distinguished Israel from all other nations, was a motive for grateful praise (Ps. 147:19f.), loyal keeping of God's law (Lev. 18:4f.), and resolute nonconformity to the idolatry and wrongdoing to the rest of the world (Lev. 18:2f.; 20:22f.; Deut. 14:1f.; Ezek. 20:5-7). It also provided Israel with grounds for unfaltering hope and trust in God in times of distress and discouragement (Isa. 41:8-14; 44:1f.; Ps. 106:4f.). (4) Within the chosen people, God chose individuals for specific tasks to further the purpose of the national election—Israel's own enjoyment of God's blessing, and, ultimately the blessing of the world. God chose Moses (Ps. 106:23), Aaron (Ps. 105:26), the priests (Deut. 18:5), the prophets (Jer. 1:5), the Kings (1 Sam. 10:24; 2 Sam. 6:21), and the Servant-Savior of Isaiah's prophecy ("My chosen," Isa. 42:1; 49:1, 5), who suffers persecution (Isa. 50:5f.), dies for sins (Isa. 53), and brings the light of salvation to the Gentiles (Isa. 42:1-7); (5) The promised blessings of election were forfeited through unbelief and disobedience.

The prophets, facing widespread hypocrisy and unbelief, insisted that God would reject the ungodly among his people (Jer. 6:30; 7:29). Numerous prophecies, with their focus on individual piety, pointed to an individualizing of the concept of election (cf. Ps. 65:4). They gave grounds for distinguishing between election to privilege and election to life, and for concluding that, while God had chosen the whole nation for the privilege of living under the covenant, he had chosen only some of them to inherit the riches of the relationship to himself which the covenant held out, while the rest forfeited those riches by their unbelief. The New Testament teaching about election assumes these distinctions (cf. Rom. 9).

The New Testament Explication

The New Testament announces the extension of God's covenant—promises to the gentile world and the transference of covenant—privileges from the lineal seed of Abraham to a predominantly gentile body (Matt. 21:43) consisting of all who had become Abraham's true seed and God's true Israel through faith in Christ (Rom. 4:9-18; 9:6f.; Gal. 3:14ff.; Eph. 2:11ff.; 3:6-8). Faithless Israel was rejected and judged, and the Christian church took Israel's place as God's chosen nation, living in the world as his people and worshiping and proclaiming him as their God.

The theological development of the idea of election is seen most clearly in the Epistles of Saint Paul. The substrative passages include Rom. 8:28—11:36; Eph. 1:3-14; 1 Thess. 1:2-10; 2 Thess. 2:13, 14; 2 Tim. 1:9, 10. From these texts we adduce the following facts: (1) Election is a gracious choice. Election by grace (Rom. 11:5; cf. 2 Tim. 1:9) is an act of undeserved favor freely shown toward members of a fallen race to which God owed nothing but wrath (Rom. 1:18ff.). (2) Election is a sovereign choice, prompted by God's own good pleasure alone (Eph. 1:5, 9) and not by any human works, accomplished or foreseen (Rom. 9:11), or any human efforts to win God's favor. Paul rehearses that it is God's election alone that explains why, when the gospel is proclaimed, some do respond. The unbelief of the rest requires no special explanation, for no sinner, left to him or herself, can believe (1 Cor. 2:14; 12:3); but the phenomenon of faith needs explaining. Saint Paul's explanation is that God by his Spirit causes people to believe, so that when they come to faith in Christ it proves their election to be a reality (1 Thess. 1:4ff.; Titus 1:1; cf. Acts 13:4-8). (3) Election is an eternal choice. God chose us, says Saint Paul, "before the foundation of the world" (Eph. 1:4; 2 Thess. 2:13; 2 Tim. 1:9). (4) Election is a choice of individual sinners to be saved in and through Christ. Election is "in Christ" (Eph. 1:4), the incarnate Son, whose historical appearing and mediation were included in God's eternal plan (1 Pet. 1:20; Acts 2:23). Election in Christ means that the elect are to be redeemed from the guilt and stain of sin by Christ, through his atoning death and the gift of his Spirit (Eph. 5:25-27; 2 Thess. 2:13; cf. 1 Pet. 1:2).

The blessings of this election are brought to the elect by means of union with Christ—his union with them representatively, as the last Adam (*Christus pro nobis*, Rom. 5:17) and vitally, as the life giver, indwelling them (*Christus in nobis*, Gal. 2:20), and their union with him by faith, a faith granted to them through God's chosen means, his Word and Sacraments (Gal. 3:26f.). (5) Saint Paul finds in the believer's knowledge of his or her election a threefold religious significance. (a) It shows that salvation, first to last, is all of God, a fruit of (sovereign) discriminating mercy. The redemption that is found in Christ alone, received by faith alone, has its source not in any personal qualification, but in grace alone. (b) It brings enduring assurance and removes all grounds for fear, and despondency. Nothing can separate a believer from the love of Christ (Rom. 8:35-39). A believer will never be safer than he is in Christ. (c) It spurs the believer to ethical endeavor. So far from sanctioning license (cf. Eph. 5:5f.) or presumption (cf. Rom. 11:19-22), the knowledge of one's election and the benefits that flow from it is the supreme incentive to humble, joyful, thankful love, the mainspring of sanctifying gratitude (Col. 3:12-17).

THE PLACE OF THE DOCTRINE OF ETERNAL ELECTION IN THEOLOGICAL STUDY

Although many position a consideration of the doctrine of eternal election among the attributes, activity (*opera ad intra*) and decrees of God, it is more properly studied after conversion, justification, and adoption. This is the juncture that most closely follows the scriptural arrangement, especially in the great New Testament doctrinal epistle, the Epistle to the Romans. Scripture does not place election at the head of the body of doctrine, nor does it make it a central doctrine that is determinative for all other doctrines. Rather, Scripture speaks of it at the end of the *ordo salutis*; more specifically it speaks of it to mature Christians who have been brought to faith by the operation of the Holy Spirit, justified, and made children of God. Saint Paul does not commence his Epistle to the Romans with a lengthy exposition of election; he follows the order of salvation, speaking first of the wrath of God against the sins of mankind (chaps. 1, 2), then of salvation through Christ alone (chap. 3), of the creation of faith and of justification (chap. 4), of the blessed consequences of justification (chap. 5), and the life that flows out of justifying faith (chaps. 6–8), before arriving at a treatment of the eternal decree and eternal predestination (chaps. 9–11). Luther wrote:

> Here we must set a boundary line for the audacious and high climbing spirits who first bring their own thinking to this matter (of election) and begin at the top to search the abyss of divine predestination and worry in vain whether they are predestined. They will certainly fall; either they will despair, or else they will take long risks. But you need to follow the order of this epistle (Romans). Worry first about Christ and the Gospel that you may recognize your sin and His grace; then fight your sin, as the first eight chapters have taught, then, when you have reached the eighth chapter and are under the cross of suffering, that will teach you the correct doctrine of predestination in the ninth, tenth, and eleventh chapters, and how comforting it is. For, in the absence of suffering and the cross and the danger of death, one cannot deal with predestination without harm and without secret offence against God. The old Adam must die before he can endure the subject and drink the strong wine of it. Therefore, beware lest you drink wine while you are yet a suckling. There is a limit, a time, an age for every doctrine.[6]

When the miracle of regeneration, justification, and adoption as God's child has been effected and the Christian, overwhelmed by the knowledge of a new-found relationship with God and deeply conscious of an inability to contribute toward securing this blessed affinity, asks: whom, in the final analysis, have I to thank for this miracle? The answer is found in the doctrine of election. When the justified child of God engages in what is frequently a losing struggle against sin, when the pressure of the world and assaults of tribulations break through, the question arises: will I be eternally saved in the face of such opposition?—once more the doctrine of election provides an answer and grants comfort.

A Lutheran Synthesis of the Doctrine of Election

Election is a "decree of God," a purpose of God definitely expressed and as definitely carried into execution: "As many as had been destined (τάσσω) for eternal life became believers" (Acts 13:48). "Just as he [God] chose (ἐκλέγω) us in Christ" (Eph. 1:4). "God chose (αἱρέω) you as the first fruits" (2 Thess. 2:13). It is also known as "predestination," each referring to the same act of God, but connoting different relations. Predestination connotes the priority of the act to the existence of those with whom it has to do. "The particle 'pre' denotes the priority of time that intervenes between the decree of predestination and the persons who are said to be predestinated; so that there is a destination of men to eternal salvation, before they were or began to be."[7]

This decree is not an absolute decree; it was not made, and is not carried out, simply in accordance with the supreme and majestic will of God (as though salvation were not the result of God's grace in Christ, but simply of an act of arbitrary choice on God's part). Rather, it is a decree in Christ; it is intimately connected with Christ and with the work of redemption wrought by Christ. "Just as he chose us in Christ" (Eph. 1:4).

It is a decree that operates through means given by God for that purpose. That is, it finds its expression not immediately, but mediately. "And those whom he predestined he also called" (Rom. 8:30) (καλέω). The call (vocation) is the announcement of God's gracious will and the provision he has made for human salvation through the mediatorial work of Christ, accompanied by the invitation to accept these blessings through faith (Matt. 22:3-9, 14). It is earnest, serious, sufficient, and efficacious; it is part of the operation of God's decree of election and is issued by and through the gospel. "For this purpose he called (καλέω) you through our proclamation of the good news" (2 Thess. 2:14).

The election of God is a decree of "grace," unmerited love and favor, a choosing, or selection that was made entirely by virtue of this attribute in God. "There is a remnant chosen (ἐκλογήν) by grace (χάριτας)" (Rom. 11:5).

There is no election, or predestination, of wrath, rejection, or damnation. Some suggest that such a decree is a necessary alternative in view of the fact that so many do not respond to the gospel invitation. But such a conclusion is untenable in the light of Scripture that knows nothing of predestination to damnation; on the contrary it declares that "God our Savior . . . desires everyone to be saved and to come to the knowledge of the truth" (1 Tim. 2:4). The unbelief of those who are lost is not the result of any decree on the part of God, but the consequence and expression of their resistance against the serious and efficacious will and intention of God pertaining to their salvation. In Antioch of Pisidia "as many as had been destined for eternal life became believers" (Acts 13:48); but of those who contradicted and blasphemed it is said: "It was necessary (ἀναγκαῖος) that the Word of God should be spoken first to you. Since you rejected it and judge yourselves to be unworthy (οὐκ ἀ ξ ίους) of eternal life, we are now turning to the Gentiles" (Acts 13:46). Obduration is not carried out upon unbelievers absolutely, but it is a recompense to them (Rom. 11:9) on account of their resistance to the gracious visitation of God in the means of grace.

The election of grace is a decree carried out in the faith and life of the Christians. The Christians' faith is not a "reason" but the "result" of the divine decree and choice. "As many as had been destined for eternal life became believers" (Acts 13:48). "God chose you as the first fruits for salvation through sanctification by the Spirit and through belief in the truth. For this purpose he called (καλέω) you through our proclamation of the good news" (2 Thess. 2:13, 14).

A further consequence of the divine election is the believer's life in agreement with the holy will of God. "Just as he chose us in Christ before the foundation of the world to be holy (ἁγίους) and blameless before him in love" (Eph. 1:4). It is clear from these texts that the election of grace, as carried out in time, is not dependent upon anything human either antecedent to a person coming to faith, or consequent to believing. God chose no person in view of his or her faith or in view of his knowledge that a certain person would come to faith or remain in the faith, or that a person would in any way be distinguished before others in accepting the grace of God offered to all in the gospel. Just as there is no cooperation on the part of humans in the act of conversion, so there is no condition, attribute, or any other factor in humans that induced God to elect them unto eternal salvation. Any theory that tries to operate with such suppositions is bound, in some measure and in some respect, to set aside the grace of God.

The election of grace has certain persons in view. The election of grace is not identical with the universal gracious will and intention of God that desires the salvation of all. Election, or choice is narrower in its function. It is the decree according to which God, from the total number of fallen people, all of whom have been redeemed by Christ and all of whom the Lord seriously desires to have saved, chooses certain ones and destines them to eternal life. The Scriptures teach that all those who are included in God's election, the election of grace, will certainly be saved. The election was not made and does not operate according to the principle: "but the one who endures to the end will be saved" (Matt. 10:22; 24:13).

This is not the election of grace. According to Scripture, God did not choose a principle, but certain persons "Just as he chose us in Christ" (Eph. 1:4). "For this purpose he called you through our proclamation of the good news" (2 Thess. 2:14). "Who are called according to his purpose" (Rom. 8:28). It is true that the word "chosen" is sometimes used figuratively (metonymy) in Scripture in addressing the believers (cf. Luke 18:7; Col. 3:12; 1 Pet. 2:9; Rev. 17:14); but this is to be understood in the same sense in which Saint Paul addresses all the members of a given congregation as "holy" and "faithful" (cf. Eph. 1:1; Col. 1:2; Phil. 1:1). All believers may thus apply the assuring words of Christ to themselves: "My sheep hear my voice. I know them, and they follow me. I give them eternal life, and they will never perish. No one will snatch them out of my hand. What my Father has given me is greater than all else, and no one can snatch it out of the Father's hand" (John 10:27-29).

Few things are more pointless and perilous than trying to determine one's election apart from Scripture. Luther wrote to some troubled souls on August 8, 1545:

> a dear friend has told me that you are at times tempted with thoughts about the predestination of God and has asked me to write this letter about this matter. Now it is true that this is a bad temptation. However, to combat it we should know that we are forbidden to understand this matter or to concern ourselves with it. For we should be glad not to know what God wants to keep secret; for this is the fruit, the eating of which brought death to Adam and Eve with all their children when they wanted to know what they were not supposed to know. Just as murdering, stealing, and cursing are sins, so it is also a sin to concern oneself with this search; and to do so is the work of the devil, as are all other sins. On the other hand, God has given us His Son, Jesus Christ; daily we should think of Him and mirror ourselves in Him. There we shall discover the predestination of God and shall find it most beautiful. For apart from Christ all is danger, death and devil; but in Him all is pure peace and joy. For after all, the person who everlastingly torments himself with thoughts about predestination gains nothing but fear. Therefore avoid and flee such thoughts as temptations that come from the serpent in Paradise. Instead look at Christ. May God have you in His keeping.[8]

Earlier (1532) Luther had written: "Staupitz (his monastic superior) consoled me with these words: 'why do you torture yourself with these speculations? Look at the wounds of Christ and at the blood He shed for you: from these your election will shine forth.' Therefore we must hear the Son of God, who was sent into the flesh and has appeared for the purpose of destroying the work of the devil and making you certain of your election. So He tells you: 'You are my sheep because you hear My voice: and no one shall pluck you out of My hands.' " And again he wrote (1538): "If you feel that you love Christ and His word and sincerely desire to remain loyal to them, let this not be a trifle to you but a sound and certain comfort that you are among the little flock that belongs to Christ and is not to be lost."[9]

Franz Pieper expressed it with his usual clarity: "Every poor sinner, therefore, who keeps his faith focused on the Gospel, without any side glances in the direction of the law, is *eo ipso* believing in his eternal election. In short, the recognition of one's election and faith in the Gospel are identical."[10]

The *Crux Theologorum*

Lutherans have been perennially aware of the impasse at which one arrives by retaining the following three teachings: the universal grace of God, the election of individuals, and the utter inability of people to contribute anything whatsoever to their conversion. Luther saw this as well, with increasing clarity, but he did not try to harmonize these teachings. He was convinced that Scripture taught all of them and was willing to bear, for the time being, the theological tension they created rather than make concessions that would violate any of them. Luther wrote:

correctly you say: If God does not desire our death, the fact that we perish must be charged to our own will. This is correct, I say, if you speak of the God who is preached; for He does want all men to be saved, because He comes to all by the Word of Salvation, and the will which does not receive Him is at fault, as He says in Matthew 23:37: "How often would I have gathered thy children together, and thou woulds't not." But why that Majesty does not take away or change this fault of our will in all persons, seeing that it is not in the power of man to do so, or why He lays to the charge of man what man cannot avoid, we are not allowed to investigate; and even though you were to investigate much, yet you would never find out, as Paul says in Romans 9:20: "Who art thou that repliest to God?"[11]

Lutherans, however, have not spoken the final word on this critical issue. Two perpetual attempts have been made to solve the mystery that appears when one contemplates this antinomy. The difference in the result, under precisely the same conditions, has been accounted for by eliminating the "same conditions" either through assuming a difference in God or by assuming a difference in those to whom the gospel is addressed. The former is the Calvinistic solution, the latter the synergistic, neither of which is acceptable to Lutherans. Calvin and, after him, the Reformed theologians generally have paralleled the decree of predestination with a decree of reprobation. By an absolute act of sovereign choice, God has from everlasting predestined certain persons to eternal life, for the glory of his love, and others to perdition for the glory of his justice.

Calvinists are divided as to where the decree of election is placed in reference to the fall (*lapsus*). Supralapsarians place the election prior to the fall thus including the fall in the elective decree; infralapsarians place the election after the fall in which case the decree appears to be focused more on human need than the majesty of God. In either case all agree that grace is not universal, but particular, and that the general preaching of the gospel is intended to be effective only in the case of the elect. Lutheran theology takes exception to this position and urges a consideration of such decisive texts as: Matt. 11:28; John 1:29; 3:16; 12:47; 2 Cor. 5:14, 15, 19; Heb. 1:9; 1 Pet. 3:9.

The other escape from the dilemma is the solution proposed by the synergists. Synergism denies, in effect, the doctrine of total depravity, and holds that in the will of the unregenerate there is a latent power that cooperates toward conversion. Thus if one person is lost while the other is saved it is because the one exerted his or her will and cooperated with the Holy Ghost whereas the other failed to do so and must suffer the consequences of this neglect. It concludes that God's election is based upon his foreknowledge of human response to the gospel invitation. For Lutherans, this teaching contravenes the entire presentation of the doctrine of election as it is seen in both the Old and New Testaments.

In conclusion, perhaps it may be wise to ponder the advice Luther offered in his oft maligned *De Servo Arbitrio*:

> Let us therefore hold in consideration the three lights, the light of nature, the light of grace, and the light of Glory. This is the

common and very good distinction. By the light of nature it is unsolvable how it can be just that the good should be afflicted and the wicked should prosper; but this is solved by the light of grace. By the light of grace it is unsolvable how God can condemn him who, by his own powers, can do nothing but sin and become guilty. Both the light of nature and the light of grace here say that the fault is not in miserable man, but in the unjust God; nor can they judge otherwise of that God who crowns the wicked freely without any merit, and yet crowns not, but condemns another, who is perhaps less, or at least not more, wicked. But the light of glory speaks otherwise and will in the hereafter show God, whose judgement now is one of incomprehensible justice, to be of the most righteous and most manifest justice. Only that we should for the time (in this life) believe it, reminded and confirmed by that example of the light of grace which accomplishes a like miracle in regard to the light of nature.[12]

Dorner in his *Geschichte der Protestantischen Theologie*, adds this comment to Luther's advice: "Luther does not assume a contradiction (between the revealed and hidden will of God); he rather suggests that one believe this contradiction to be only a seeming one."

Article XI of the Formula of Concord points Lutherans in a proper direction; instead of seeking to fathom the mystery of election-predestination or suggesting a logically flawless system it merely asserts: (a) If we hear and believe and are saved, it is due *entirely* to God's elective grace, and (b) if we do not believe, fall into unbelief, and are lost it is *entirely* our own fault. This is not "logical" as we ordinarily use the term, but it is strictly in line with the real inner nature of faith. Faith gives all glory to God. The man who believes finds the source of everything good in God, not in himself, but the source of evil in himself, and not in God.[13]

REFORMULATIONS OF THE DOCTRINE SINCE LUTHER AND CALVIN

While the doctrine of election became a pivotal article in the Reformed tradition, it remained a controversial one. In the course of this controversy, Calvin's celebrated admission that he found the decree concerning reprobation "horrible" was often cited.[14] But in his own case and in that of his followers, this admission did not reflect a sadistic turn of mind but an unshakable conviction that double predestination was the plain teaching of Scripture. Such reasoning did not, however, satisfy all, even though they accepted the authority of Scripture. In Holland, where the doctrine was given its most vigorous defense, it also suffered its most vigorous rejection in the writings of Jacobus Arminius, which have come to be known as Arminianism. Citing the twentieth question of the Heidelberg Catechism, that not all who perish in Adam are saved but only those who "by true faith are engrafted into Christ and embrace all His benefits," Arminius comments. "From this sentence I infer that God has not absolutely predestined any to salvation; but that He has in His decree considered (or looked upon) them as believers."[15] Pursuing such reasoning, Arminius came to the conclusion that God foresees the choice the sinner will make and bases his own choice thereon. Hence, he maintained that every scheme of predestination, and particularly supralapsarianism, subverts the gospel.

After much controversy in the decade following Arminius's death, five articles were drawn up by his followers under the name of Remonstrance. At the Synod of Dort (1618) the Dutch church not only rejected the Arminian articles but affirmed five counterdoctrines that the Arminians rejected in turn. These doctrines came to be known as the "Five points of Calvinism" (commonly remembered with the help of the acronym TULIP: (1) total depravity, (2) unconditional election, (3) limited atonement, (4) irresistible grace, and (5) perseverance of the saints. Though the debate with the Remonstrants principally concerned the doctrines related to predestination, other items in Arminius's thoughts were also discussed and rejected. Though generally forgotten long since, some of these items anticipated the radical departure of his followers from orthodoxy. Arminius, for example, defended the thesis "It is a new, heretical and Sabellian mode of speaking, nay it is blasphemous to say with Calvin, that the Son of God is *homoousios* (very God), for the Father alone is very God, not the Son or the Spirit," and again, "The righteousness of Christ is not imputed to us for righteousness, as Luther contended, but to believe (or the act of believing) justifies us."[16]

As the first major spokesman for Protestant liberalism, Schleiermacher (1768–1834) restated the doctrine of predestination in a significant way. He understood election to mean in accordance with the laws of divine government, those living on earth at one time are never uniformly taken up into the kingdom of God. When individuals are taken up into that kingdom, each in his or her own turn, this is "simply the result of the fact that the justifying divine activity is in manifestation determined by, and forms part of, the general government of the world. . . . And since the whole government of the world is, like the world itself, eternal in God, nothing happens in the kingdom of grace without foreordination."[17] But the fact that there are those in whom God's predestination has not attained its true end (blessedness in Christ) does not allow us to conclude that for some there may be a predestination to reprobation. This would result in "an insoluble discord" and in Schleiermacher's system there is no room for "insoluble discords." We thus conclude that there will be universal salvation based on a single predestination for all—the election to life. "If we proceed," he writes, "on the assumption that all belonging to the human race are eventually taken up into living fellowship with Christ, there is nothing but this single divine foreordination."[18]

Perhaps the most influential theologian of this century has been Karl Barth, a spokesman for the Swiss Reformed church. In fundamental sympathy with the Augustinian position that salvation is the gift of God's electing grace rather than a reward for human merit, Barth nonetheless felt constrained to reject the traditional form in which the doctrine of predestination had been cast. Though he found it hard to believe, he became convinced that even such consummate theological minds as Saint Augustine, Thomas Aquinas, and Calvin had erred in their formulations of this doctrine. He believed the nature of their mistake was that they divorced God from Jesus Christ—that is to say, when they thought of God's election, they thought abstractly of the eternal decree of the hidden God rather than concretely of the gracious purpose of the God revealed in Jesus Christ. As a result, they missed the decisive insight into the heart of the matter which has to do with the question of the object of predestination (*objectum praedestinationis*). All concerned parties assumed that the object of the decree was a fixed number of elect and reprobate individuals. Barth maintained that if the theologians had thought of election and reprobation in terms of God's eternal purpose in Jesus Christ, they would have perceived that the answer to the election-reprobation question lies in him. He is the electing God who has become the elect man—not "an" elect man among many but "the" elect man. All individual men and women are elect in him, the second Adam, in whom all are alive (1 Cor. 15:22). But his election, unlike ours, is unto death, that we who deserve death might enjoy eternal life. As the one predestined to death, he is the one true reprobate. When we speak of Christ's death, says Barth, we speak of the "shadow side of predestination." Predestination, then, is double, since Christ is both the elect man and the reprobate man. Double predestination in this sense, so far from being a *decretum horribile,* is really good news, since it tells us that he stands in our place as the reprobate while we, because we are elect in him, have eternal life. This is the sum of the gospel. Thus election becomes the best of all words that can be said or heard, for it testifies to the free unchanging grace of God, a grace to which witness is born in all his works.[19]

Barth's effort has been praised as a breakthrough, a brilliant stroke that cuts the Gordian knot of the age-old predestinarian problem. Where there was darkness, there is now light; where there was mystery there is now good news. It did not take long, however, for some theologians to perceive that Barth had solved one problem (reprobation) by introducing another (restitutionism, *apokatastasis*). If all are elect in Christ by an eternal decree, then it would seem that no negative decision at the human level (unbelief) could ever frustrate the prior positive decision at the divine level (election). Hence, all will be saved in the end. Although Barth did not draw that inference, or teach it, the criticism lingers.

Emil Brunner, Barth's colleague in the Swiss Reformed church, also attempted to find a new formulation of the doctrine of election.[20] He taught that historic Calvinism teaches determinism: and if we add the doctrine of reprobation, we get an ironclad determinism. We can neither love nor believe in a God like that. But, continued Brunner, that which Calvin and associates were trying to say is correct, namely, that God does elect in Christ, that people do depend upon the grace and initiative of God, that nothing in humans merits salvation. He defines election as follows:

> Thus it is this revealed eternity alone, through which, and in which, I, this individual human being, this individual person, receive eternal meaning, and my individual personal existence is taken seriously. In the Christian revelation of eternity my eyes are opened to perceive the truth that God, My *Lord,* regards *me* from all eternity, with the gaze of everlasting love, and therefore that my individual personal existence and life now receive an eternal meaning. The call that is addressed to me through Jesus Christ from all eternity calls me to my eternal destiny. To be called from the eternity of God to eternal communion with God—that is the Gospel of Jesus Christ. Briefly,

that is the meaning of the New Testament message of eternal election.[21]

It is the address of the gospel to me through the Holy Spirit whereby "we *ought* to believe, we are *able* to believe, and we *must* believe."[22] Furthermore Brunner states that the older doctrine had a false doctrine of eternity. Its doctrine of causality is that God treats humans like a rock or a tree trunk. The biblical doctrine of causality is totally personal, or existential. The older doctrine of eternity spoke about a pre-temporal decree of God. But eternity is a dimension of present reality. From this eternity God chooses me and confronts me with the eternal meaning of my life.

Brunner agrees with Barth's treatment of election insofar as it rejects the older view and attempts a new formulation. But Brunner also disagrees. First, he argues that Barth's doctrine is so thoroughly objective that it diminishes the spiritual and existential character of the believer and Jesus Christ. Second, he argues that in Barth's doctrine Christ is the reprobate or rejected one, which means that no other person can be rejected, hence all will be saved. Brunner states that the witness of Scripture is very clear, that there is a day of final judgment with an eternal division of humankind into saved and lost.

For the past 100 years an ongoing debate within Lutheranism has focused on whether or not the elective decree is based on the *intuitu fidei* (or *intuitu fidei finalis*). Holding this position have been prominent theologians from the former American Lutheran Church (Joseph Stump *et alii*) and the Lutheran Church in America (Henry Jacobs *et alii*) while the Missouri Synod, led by C. F. W. Walther and Franz Pieper, has been adamantly opposed to it. During the debate, Missouri was accused by its opponents of being crypto-Calvinists, whereas Missouri saw in the *intuitu fidei* position a form of implicit synergism. At present the debate is rarely aired beyond the confines of the seminary classroom.

A recent Fortress Press publication includes a very stimulating division (the index lists the divisions as "loci") by Robert W. Jenson, a theologian of the Evangelical Lutheran Church in America (ELCA) in which he presents a suggestive reformulation of the doctrine of predestination.[23] Jenson begins by saying, "Predestination is simply the doctrine of justification stated in the active voice. If we change 'We are justified by God alone' from passive to active we get 'God alone justifies us.' "[24] This divine monergism leads us to realize the impossibility of free will. "If there is the God of the Bible, there can be no such thing as the free will (*liberum arbitrium*) of traditional discussion."[25] It also pilots us toward a recognition of two absolute wills of God not easily interpreted as the same. "If God wills all things, God in some way wills Auschwitz and the torture of the child in Ivan Karamazov's fable, and the damnation of the damned if God chooses. How is that to be reconciled with the revelation of God's will in the Gospel as a 'fountain of sheer love?' "[26] Jenson continues, "It is this threatening split in our image of God which is the true religious occasion of theological history's many attempts to mitigate the assertion of predestination. These run from semi-Pelagianism . . . through such devices as the teaching (shared by Jesuits and most Lutherans from 1600 on) that God eternally pre-ordains to salvation those who God foresees will by free choice believe the gospel when it is preached to them. . . .

> Instead of such evasions, what is needed is the insight that God's general rule of creation is not the appropriate primary context in which to interpret the particular absoluteness of the Gospel's God. The necessary step from the dominant tradition is recognition that our predestination is not the act of a God-the-Father abstracted from the triune relations, sorting fates in a pretemporal eternity. It occurs rather as the act in time of Christ's death and resurrection and of the proclamation of the gospel. When someone speaks to me the promises made by Christ's resurrection, that event is the event of God's choice about me. Such a christological and hermeneutic understanding of predestination first emerged in early Lutheranism, but it was carried to systematic reflection only by Karl Barth: "Precisely Jesus Christ is himself God's act of election, and therefore God's word, decision and beginning." Since Jesus Christ is a personal reality, it is only an alternate formulation: "Jesus Christ is the electing God."[27]

Jenson moves on to develop his own restatement, noting that the christological interpretation is the first step from the traditional position but it cannot be the last. He says:

> We will be able rightly to interpret the unity of God's absolute will only if we make Spirit-discourse rather than Father-discourse or Son-discourse—the primary locus of our interpretation. It is indeed the human Christ's temporal address to us that is the event of God's eternal choosing about us. . . . But the eternity of this moment must be established not by the

prefix "pre" but by the prefix "post": it is in that the man Christ *will* be the agent and center of the final community, that his will for us is the eternal determination of our lives. The Trinitarian dialectics can be the appropriate conceptual scheme of predestination only if the whole scheme—of Father, Son *and* Spirit—is affirmed. The speaking of the gospel is the event of predestination in that the gospel gives what it speaks about, but this eschatological efficacy of the gospel in the Spirit is the choosing God.[28]

He sums it up:

If we interpret predestination as the work of the Spirit, the Power of the future, we will leave off such synthesis (a harmony of the two wills of God). How the God of the gospel and the Will behind all events can be one is—we will say—the one truth about God reserved for the End, when we shall see God face to face.[29]

In the final assessment Jenson ends up where Luther does— the antinomy remains with us *ad finem.* Only when we perceive with the clarity of the "light of Glory," as Luther contends, or at the point of Jenson's *visio Dei beatifica* will all be resolved. So let Luther speak our concluding word as he writes, on April 30, 1531, to Barbara Lischner who was troubled and concerned about her election:

Among all the commands of God the foremost is that we should place His dear Son, our Lord Jesus Christ, before us. He must be the daily and foremost Mirror for our hearts. In Him we see how, as a good God, He has so thoroughly provided for us that He even gave His dear Son for us. Here, here, I say, one really learns to understand predestination, and nowhere else. You will note that you believe in Christ. But if you believe, you are called; if you are called, you surely are also predestinated. Let this mirror and throne of grace not be taken away from your mind's eye. But when such thoughts of rejection come to you and bite like fiery serpents, then whatever you do, pay no attention to these thoughts or serpents, but turn your eyes away from them and look at the brazen serpent, that is, at Christ, who was given for us. Then, God willing, matters will be better. But, as stated, we must fight and constantly rid ourselves of these thoughts of doubt. If they come to you, let them go away, just as you would quickly spit out any mud that may fall into your mouth.[30]

8

The New Testament
Concept of Election

RESPONSE TO FREDERICK HARM'S
"ELECTION: A LUTHERAN-BIBLICAL VIEW"

Frederick Harm has presented a lucid and comprehensive overview of predestination and election from a Lutheran point of view. He has addressed the difficult issues of divine omnipotence and human freedom, the problem of synergy, and the charge that Missouri Synod Lutheranism tends toward a Calvinistic understanding of election. His comments on the Calvinist-Arminian controversy clearly illustrate how different theological presuppositions can lead to incompatible interpretations of key scriptural passages.

The following pages attempt to indicate points at which an Orthodox understanding of election and predestination (with the related issue of synergy) differs from the one he presents.

A SUMMARY OF DIFFERENCES

Reading through Frederick Harm's paper, I was struck by certain affirmations that seem to distort the biblical witness. The result is an understanding of predestination that seriously jeopardizes human freedom and responsibility. Such affirmations include: (1) the introductory quote, "God before the foundation of the world chose us in his Son Jesus Christ out of the mass of sinful mankind unto faith. . . ," together with the distinction between "election to privilege" and "election to life" (p. 135); (2) the statement, "Saint Paul's explanation is that God by his Spirit *causes* people to believe" (p.

136, italics mine); (3) the statement, "Just as there is no cooperation on the part of humans in the act of conversion, so there is no condition, attribute, or any other factor in humans that induced God to elect them unto eternal salvation" (p. 140); (4) the exclusivism expressed by the notion of "election of grace" that holds, ". . . God, from the total number of fallen people, all of whom have been redeemed by Christ and all of whom the Lord seriously desires to have saved, chooses certain ones and destines them to eternal life" (p. 140); and (5) synergism defined (according to an Arminian rather than an Eastern patristic view) in opposition to the doctrine of total depravity, concluding that "in the will of the unregenerate there is a latent power that cooperates toward conversion" (p. 143).

Orthodoxy would take issue with these points in the following way. While affirming that all persons are fallen and all are redeemed in Christ, Orthodoxy insists that *all* are free to share in the fruits of Christ's saving work through faith, repentance, and love. The human will is tainted by the fall (thus the patristic distinction between the "gnomic," or personal will, and the "natural," or essential will). This does not, however, eliminate human responsibility for cooperation with God in the process of salvation. The alternative is not "bondage of the will" or a Pelagian notion that we can literally "work out our own salvation." Synergy does not imply (as Arminius seems to think it does) that "in the will of the unregenerate there is a latent power which co-operates toward conversion." It means rather an attitude of openness in faith to the saving grace of God. As such, it always follows, and never precedes, the divine initiative.

Synergy cannot be understood as an autonomous human action that adds some indispensable element to the formula for salvation. Against both Calvinism and Arminianism, Orthodoxy understands synergy as open receptivity in faith and love to God's gracious act; fully, uniquely, and perfectly realized through the crucifixion of Christ and his ascension into glory. All initiative in salvation belongs to God, who alone is its "efficient cause."

With regard to the work of God, we can affirm that divine initiative precedes human response. All saving work is accomplished by God in Christ; even human response in faith and love derive from divine initiative, through the indwelling Spirit (Rom. 5:5; 1 John 3:24; 4:13; etc.). From the side of human creatures, synergy means free acceptance of God's saving grace, demanding response, despite human "weakness" (cf. Rom. 8:26); it includes our witness to the world, to proclaim the freely received gift of life—a witness borne through faith, works of love, and martyrdom; and it involves us in "spiritual combat," which means striving toward restoration of the *imago dei*—again, in the power of the indwelling Spirit—described variously as sanctification, perfection, or deification.

Thus the Orthodox affirm, with Lutherans, that we are totally incapable of saving ourselves or even contributing actively to the work of salvation. Synergy or cooperation is restricted to our response to grace, a response possible because the human will is not in total bondage but remains sufficiently free to "seek first the kingdom of God." That seeking, however, is a gift of grace; longing for the kingdom is a God-given longing. We can only love God because God first loved us and offered his Son for our salvation (1 John 4:9).

Confusion arises when the accent is placed exclusively on the matter of "will," leading to the false alternative, "free or depraved?" The key element in human response to divine, saving grace is not the exercise of will; more fundamental is the attitude of repentance, "a broken and contrite heart" that can, by the power of the Spirit, render even a fallen and rebellious (gnomic) will capable of accepting the free gift of life.

Synergy implies a fundamental antinomy: a person must accept God's grace to be saved (through an exercise of free will); but such acceptance is only possible through the sanctifying power of the Spirit. As Dr. Harm points out (p. 135), "the promised blessings of election [in Israel] were forfeited through unbelief and disobedience." Election can be voided by acts of unrighteousness and faithlessness. Predestination is not absolute. Freedom of the will is manifest in the coming to faith and in the sinful rejection of grace. Therefore, we cannot say, "God causes humans [us] to believe." Neither incipient belief nor mature faith is imposed by the Spirit. Both are our responsibility. Nevertheless, "by grace you [we] have been saved through faith, and this is not your [our] own doing; it is the gift of God" (Eph. 2:8) apart from works, merits, or any other accomplishment of our own. Although the antinomy remains intact, it does not vitiate human freedom.

SCRIPTURE AND THE DOCTRINE OF ELECTION OR PREDESTINATION

Thus Orthodoxy would reject the Lutheran doctrine of the "bondage of the will," as it would the Calvinist doctrine of "total depravity." Consequently it would also reject any doctrine of "selective predestination," implying that "God before the foundation of the world chose us . . . out of the mass of sinful mankind."[1] The doctrine of election or predestination, as presented here, seems rooted in a misinterpretation of the key scriptural passages used to support it. A careful reading of the following texts indicates that "election" does not refer to salvation, but to *mission:* God "predestines" or "elects" some to constitute the body of Christ, the church, in order that the church might fulfill Israel's vocation to bring the message of the gospel to all the world (Matt. 28:16-20).

The following passages are summarized from Graebner's list in Frederick Harm's paper, p. 133.

"An Eternal Act of God"

Eph. 1:4. This passage must be read in the context of 1:3-10 which concludes in verse 10, "to gather up all things [*ta panta*] in him." This implies universal outreach. Here "election" is the apostolic ministry of unity, to be assumed by all who are baptized. The "we" who are chosen are the Jews who first came to Christ; the "you" are the Gentiles who receive the gospel through their witness. The distinction is definitely not between "us" and "the mass of sinful human beings," for "all have sinned and fall short of the glory of God" (Rom. 3:23).

2 Thess. 2:13. Chapter 2:10-12 distinguishes between those who accept and those who reject the gospel, based on free choice. Those who reject it are afflicted by God with "delusion," but only after their act of rejection, "so that all who have not believed the truth but took pleasure in unrighteousness might be condemned." Verse 2:13 reads *aparchēn eis sōterian* (BFG, etc.), meaning that "God chose you as the first fruits [of many]." Although RSV reads *ap' archēs,* implying selective election ("God chose you from the beginning . . ."), this easier reading is to be rejected as secondary.[2] Here there is no notion of "selective predestination."

2 Tim. 1:9. God saved and called us for his purpose and by grace rather than on the basis of our works. Like Rom. 9:11, this simply refutes the idea of salvation through works of the law (merits).

"Who for His Goodness Sake"

Rom. 11:15. *Apobolē* does not mean "rejection" [of the Jews], since that would contradict verse one. It must be translated "set aside," implying "for a time," "until the full number of Gentiles has come in. And so all Israel will be saved" (Rom. 11:25f.).

"Because of the Merit of the . . . Redeemer"

Eph. 3:11. This verse refers simply to the "eternal purpose that he [God] has carried out in Jesus Christ our Lord" and revealed through the church. There is no notion of predestination here.

"Everlasting Life"

Acts 13:48. A current Jewish expression in New Testament times is *hosoi ēsan tetagmenoi eis zoēn aiōnion.* It does not imply predestination as shown by Acts 13:46—belief in or rejection of the gospel is a matter of free choice. *Tetagmenoi* refers to divine foreknowledge.

2 Tim. 2:10. Paul endures "everything for the sake of the elect, so that they may also obtain the salvation that is in Christ Jesus." The "elect" must be saved by the apostle's preaching. Nothing is automatic; there is no selective predestination. This is confirmed by the "ifs" found in 2:11-13).

Rom. 8:28-30. The word *proōrisen* implies called, foreknew, predestined. In this context Paul assures those who are weak, but who love God, that God foreknew and predestined them to be conformed to the image of Christ and justified; they are already glorified, bearing the first fruits of the Spirit. Paul concludes the chapter by pointing out that "if God is for us, who is against us?" (vv. 31ff.). Election is a consequence of God's foreknowledge. Paul's message is this: "God is in control," equivalent to the gospel "revelatory phrase" *egō eimi, mē phobeisthe* (e.g., John 6:20).

"Salvation Designated for All"

1 Pet. 1:2. In the Revised Standard Version, this verse reads "[elect of the diaspora] chosen and destined by God the Father. . . ." The Greek text translates it: *[eklektois] kata prognōsin theou patros.* Like Eph. 1:4 and other verses, it refers to God's plan laid up from before creation. There is no notion of an elect group over against the sinful world. In First Peter election always reflects Christ's eternal election. First Peter 1:20 and 2:9 show that this refers to the mission of those chosen.

"A Certain Number"

Matt. 20:16. "The last will be first, and the first will be last" does not refer to predestination. Who is first and last depends on individual decision or choice, on whether or not a person accepts the gospel message. Those who are first in this world are last in the kingdom, implying ethical criteria for salvation (cf. Matt. 19:30; Luke 13:30). All people have the option of faith (sealed by works of love) to be first in the kingdom.

Matt. 22:14. "For many are called, but few are chosen" shows a distinction between *klētoi* and *eklektoi.* "Many" is a Semitism for "all" (cf. Matt. 26:28, "blood . . . poured out for many"). Those "called" are not limited to a select few, "a certain number" among "the mass of sinful people." All are called; if only a few enter the kingdom ("the chosen"/admitted, received, welcomed) it is because the others do not properly respond to God's free invitation (they put on no "wedding garment"). Only those whose faith and conduct conform to Christ (cf. the parables of Matt. 25: talents, last judgment) are welcomed into the feast. This does not imply predestination of a certain number. God invites all; those who are excluded exclude themselves.

"Of Certain Persons"

2 Tim. 2:19. This verse refers only to God's foreknowledge and to human response (cf. Num. 16:5, 26; Isa. 26:13). Numbers 16:5 does refer to God's election, but serves only to legitimate the Levites over against those of Korah's rebellion; whereas the latter two refer to an individual's free response. But this does not support "election of certain persons" as distinct from the invitation God extends to all.

John 13:18. "I know whom I have chosen" (together with verse 20) shows by the contrast between Judas and the Eleven, that election depends upon one's response to Christ: "whoever receives. . . ." Again, election concerns those who respond in faith; but there is never any hint that their response is determined by God ("caused by the Spirit"). Free will remains intact.

"To Procure . . . Final Salvation"

The passages under this heading concern only "God's eternal purpose in Jesus Christ." Mark 13:20-22 shows that the "elect" are by definition those who are faithful, implying a response in faith and obedience.

THE NEED FOR FURTHER IN-DEPTH STUDY OF SCRIPTURE

In the New Testament "election" or "predestination" cannot be construed to imply that some, and only some, out of the mass of sinful mankind are chosen by God for eternal life (implying, even if it is not stated, that the rest of humanity is lost). God extends an invitation to all, Jew and Gentile alike, to enter the kingdom through faith in the saving work of his Son. The "elect" are those who accept God's free invitation, manifesting faith and performing the righteous works that confirm that faith.

It seems that the terms "election" and "predestination" have been misinterpreted to imply that God predetermines our faith and obedience (the Spirit causes us to believe). This is due to the confusion between the terms "foreknowledge" and "determinism." As with the problem of theodicy, we ask how we can reconcile the image of an omniscient and omnipotent God of love with the image of humans possessed of free will. We deduce the following: God is omniscient (he knows all things). Therefore God knows from all eternity who will accept the gospel (leading to life) or reject the gospel (leading to death). God is omnipotent (he determines all things by his sovereign will). Therefore God must will from all eternity those who number among the elect and the damned.

As rationally coherent as this conclusion might be, it leads inevitably to what Calvin himself called the "horrible" implications of the doctrine of double predestination. Somehow divine foreknowledge and human freedom must be reconciled without introducing the element of deterministic predestination, which selects only an elect few while admitting that all people have been reconciled and saved in Christ. We can only resolve the problem by preserving both poles of an irreducible antinomy: God knows from eternity who will and who will not accept the gospel message and receive the gift of life; but he does not determine their decision for faith or unfaith. In Frederick Harm's formulation, "Election is a sovereign choice . . . [yet] a choice of individual sinners to be saved in and through Christ" (p. 136). Divine foreknowledge and human freedom must be held together, for both are true.

In the New Testament "election" refers either to that divine foreknowledge or to the selection of those who are chosen for a universal mission, that the gospel might be preached "to the ends of the earth." It never implies that human freedom is suspended so that God alone determines who numbers among the saved. For the "non-elect" can always and at any moment become numbered among the elect through repentance and faith, just as the "elect" can void their election by rejecting faith and working unrighteousness. To deny that possibility on the grounds of predestination introduces a mechanistic determinism into the economy of salvation, which reduces to empty rhetoric the call of Christ to "repent and believe."

While Lutherans and Orthodox agree on the basic question of salvation by grace and not by works, there remains significant disagreement on the question of election and predestination. The disagreement is due less to differences in doctrinal stance than to the ways we interpret biblical, and especially New Testament passages that use the language of "election" and "predestination." Speaking as just one Orthodox student of the Scriptures, I find no grounds in the biblical text for affirming that "God chose us out of the mass of sinful mankind," or that the Spirit "causes man to believe." The Lutheran position, so well put forth in Frederick Harm's paper, seems to affirm both because of its adherence to the teaching of "the bondage of the will" and its rejection of a "synergy" that is more Arminian than Orthodox.

If, by the grace of God, the fruitful work we have begun can continue—whether by our group or another—perhaps the chief focus should be on joint, passage-by-passage exegesis of the texts in question. By returning to the biblical sources, we should be able to move beyond the narrowly conceived doctrinal positions we hold on matters such as election and synergy, and discover the revealed truth that unites us in our Lord Jesus Christ.

9

Predestination According to Divine Foreknowledge in Patristic Tradition

The predestination of the just to eternal glory is a truth of the Christian faith that is professed in both Holy Scripture and Church Tradition. In the deepest sense of the word, predestination is a theological mystery beyond our human ability to comprehend totally. It balances two equally valid principles: God's divine foreknowledge and sovereign will, and human freedom and moral responsibility.

SACRED SCRIPTURE

Holy Scripture clearly teaches the predestination of the saints. Our Lord Jesus Christ, in his eschatological discourse, states that at the last judgment "the king will say to those at his right hand, 'Come, you that are blessed by my Father, inherit the kingdom prepared for you from the foundation of the world' " (Matt. 25:34). Elsewhere Jesus consoles his disciples, "rejoice that your names are written in heaven" (Luke 10:20), and that of the sheep entrusted to him, "No one will snatch them out of my hand" (John 10:28).

The predestination by God of the just to eternal glory is also a cardinal affirmation of the holy apostle Paul. God "saved us and called us with a holy calling, not according to our works but according to his own purpose and grace. This grace was given to us in Christ Jesus before the ages began" (2 Tim. 1:9). Paul thus salutes the Ephesians: God "chose us in Christ before the foundation of the world to be holy and blameless before him in love. He destined

159

(προορίσας) us for adoption as his children through Jesus Christ, according to the good pleasure (εὐδοκίαν) of his will, to the praise of his glorious grace that he freely bestowed on us in the Beloved. . . . With all wisdom and insight he has made known to us the mystery (μυστήριον/ *sacramentum*) of his will, according to his good pleasure that he set forth in Christ, as a plan (οἰκονομίαν) for the fullness of time, to gather up (ἀνακεφαλαιώσασθαι) all things in him, things in heaven and things on earth. In Christ we have also obtained an inheritance (ἐκληρώθημεν), having been destined (προορ-ισθέντες) according to the purpose (πρόθεσιν) of him who accomplishes all things according to his counsel and will" (Eph. 1:4-11).

The locus classicus for Paul's doctrine about the predestination by God of the just to eternal glory is accorded to us in the Epistle to the Romans (8:28-30): "We know that all things work together (συνεργεῖ) for good for those who love God, who are called (κλητοῖς) according to his purpose. For those whom he foreknew (προέγνω) he also predestined (προώρισεν) to be conformed to the image of his Son, in order that he might be the firstborn within a large family. And those whom he predestined he also called; and those whom he called he also justified; and those whom he justified he also glorified (οὓς δὲ προώρισεν, τούτους καὶ ἐκάλεσεν καὶ οὓς ἐκάλεσεν, τούτους καὶ ἐδικαίωσεν οὓς δὲ ἐδικαίωσεν, τούτους καὶ ἐδόξασεν).

The nuances of the Pauline texts on predestination have been examined by Scripture commentators throughout the centuries.[1] We shall not concern ourselves with a thorough analysis of the scriptural texts. Instead, we shall focus on the interpretations of these texts by church theologians, which led to both the convergence and the divergence over the question of predestination in Christian tradition.

SAINT AUGUSTINE AND PELAGIANISM

In our investigation of church tradition concerning the mystery of predestination, we shall begin *in medias res*, so to speak, with Saint Augustine's clear expostulation of his understanding of predestination when he was confronted with the heresy of Pelagianism. After examining how later Western Christians addressed the question of predestination, we shall return to the writings of the Greek fathers and the pre-Augustinian Latin fathers. Their observations afford us an insight into the mystery of predestination, the dimensions of which were not predetermined by the polarization between Pelagianism andAugustinianism that has captured the attention of Western medieval and Reformation authorities from that time to the present.

At the beginning of the fifth century, while the Christian East was engulfed in Trinitarian and christological controversies, a new heresy made its appearance in the West. It was entirely unlike the ones previously known in the East. This heresy, known as Pelagianism, involved the fields of Christian anthropology and soteriology. Its protagonist, the British lay-monk Pelagius, proposed an overly optimistic view of human nature and asserted that the individual can take the initial and fundamental steps toward salvation without the necessary assistance of divine grace.

Saint Augustine immediately and correctly perceived that Pelagianism was not simply an abstract theory, but that it eviscerated God's redemptive activity in the incarnation, death, and resurrection of his Son. Saint Augustine was overwhelmingly conscious of the sins of his early life and that God's merciful grace and love alone effected his conversion. He expressed himself so unsurpassingly in the Prologue to his confessions, "Tu excitas, ut laudare te delectet, quia fecisti nos ad te et inquietum est cor nostrum, donec requiescat in te." "*Tu* excitas—*You* stir us up and awaken us!"—the initiative must be on God's part. Although Augustine often addressed the issues of grace, justification, free will, predestination, and election, it was under the impulse of Pelagianism that the thoughts of the mature Augustine were set forth. Three works in particular, written near the end of Augustine's life, contain his central themes on predestination: *De dono perseverantiae*, *De praedestionatione sanctorum*, and *De correptione et gratia*.[2]

Saint Augustine defined predestination as "the foreknowledge and preparation of the favors of God by which all those who are set free are set free with certainty."[3] Predestination is the vocation and election not only to grace but also to glory, containing the gift of perseverance (*donum perseverantiae*): "God wills to give to the elect the grace to persevere until the end—this is what Paul means when he says 'For it is God who works in you, both to will and to work for his good pleasure' " (Phil. 2:13).[4]

Predestination depends, not on human response and acceptance, but on the eternal decree of God. Thus, for Saint Augustine, God's foreknowledge of human merits and sins was not the cause of predestination. The sovereign and non-frustratable will of God was the basis of predestination: "There is no doubt that human will cannot resist the will of God, who has done whatsoever He willed in heaven and on earth, in that He does what He wills and when He wills. Undoubtedly He has the power to move the human heart to submit, as it pleases Him, to His omnipotent will."[5] Saint Augustine expressed himself in a similar way elsewhere: "There is no doubt that we will whenever we will, but He is the cause of our willing what is good. . . . There is no doubt that we act whenever we act, but He is the cause of our acting, by most efficaciously strengthening our will."[6]

The divine will to predestination and election is not unjust. Since all men, from their birth, have inherited guilt through the sin of Adam[7] and belong to the *massa damnata*, God, without any injustice, can allow certain souls to perish in their state of corruption without according them the grace of justification:

> For as many as are set free by the grace of God from this lineage (of Adam) are likewise set free from damnation, by which they were held bound. Wherefore, if no one would be set free, nobody would reprehend the just judgment of God. While they are few in comparison with those who perish, yet in their own true number many are set free. It happens by grace, it happens gratuitously, and graces operate because it happens.[8]

Saint Augustine confessed that the mystery of predestination is beyond human capacity to comprehend. The only answer lies in the inscrutable will of God:

> Of two children equally held captive by original sin, why is one taken and the other left? Of two wicked persons already advanced in years, why is one called and the other not? These are the inscrutable judgments of God *(inscrutabilia sunt judicia Dei)*. And of two pious persons, why is perseverance until the end given to one, and not given to the other? These are the more inscrutable judgments of God *(inscrutabiliora sunt judicia Dei)*.[9]

And likewise: "Why God draws this one and not that one, seek not to judge, if you wish not to err."[10]

For Saint Augustine, predestination presupposed a decisive and definitive will on God's part to sanctify and save freely all the elect.[11] He realized that his theory of predestination ran counter to 1 Tim. 2:4, that God "desires all men to be saved." How could one speak about a universal salvific will, since God is omnipotent, and if he willed the salvation of all people, then all would be saved. We know that Saint Augustine's thinking on this matter underwent modification during his lifetime. Before he became bishop (396), he held to the universal salvific will, and he explained the fact that some believe while others do not by saying that this was due to their will or refusal to believe. Then around the year 397, in a letter addressed to Bishop Simplicianus of Milan,[12] Saint Augustine explained that, after a more thorough study of the Epistle to the Romans, he became more convinced about the omnipotence of the divine will. In this light, he came to the conclusion that God's will to save is a particular and not a universal will. The difference between the believer and the unbeliever, the good and the bad, the saved and the lost, was to be ascribed to the divine will in their regard. Thus, within this context, Saint Augustine's exegesis of 1 Tim. 2:4 was forced: all who are saved are saved because God wills it, or God desires that we wish all people to be saved.[13] Saint Augustine, therefore, was aware that this Pauline text did not fit in with his notion of predestination based on the sovereign divine will. While Saint Augustine strongly asserted the positive predestination of the elect to glory, the non-elect, the reprobate, were hopelessly lost because they lacked the necessary grace.[14]

POST-AUGUSTINIAN DEVELOPMENT IN THE WEST

The controversies over grace and predestination did not cease with the death of the Bishop of Hippo in 430. The discussions continued, especially in southern Gaul. The monks of Marseilles and Lerins (to whom it was that Saint Augustine addressed his treatises *De gratia et libero arbitrio* and *De correptione et gratia* for their instruction), under the leadership of abbot John Cassian of Saint Victor, were equally disturbed by Saint Augustine's formulation of predestination as well as the Pelagian notion of grace as an assistance for humans, but not necessary for salvation. The Massilian monks ascribed to the universal salvific will, and they were of the persuasion that grace did not depend directly on the will of God, but on his foreknowledge of a person's good or evil deeds (*praevisa merita*). Nevertheless, we can draw the conclusion that they did revert to the heresy of Pelagianism by teaching that the *initium fidei*, the first step toward salvation, can be human work, while still maintaining that the work cannot be perfected without divine grace.[15]

The defenders of Saint Augustine, who rose to the occasion, were Prosper of Aquitaine, Fulgentius of Ruspe, and Caesarius of

Arles. In most instances a faithful disciple of Augustine, Prosper modified two of the more extreme elements in his master's teaching: he stressed God's foreknowledge of human merits and demerits, and he parted with Augustine by reaffirming the universal salvific will of God:

> We must most sincerely believe and profess that God wills all men to be saved. For this indeed is the mind of the Apostle (1 Tim. 2:4), who most urgently commands what is a most devout custom in all the churches, that suppliant prayers be offered to God for all men. That many of these perish is the fault of those who perish; that many are saved is the gift of Him who saves.[16]

These two schools of thought, the moderate Augustinians and the Massilians (later somewhat inaccurately dubbed semi-Pelagians), continued the debate over grace and predestination for the next century. This uniquely Western controversy was the impetus for the convocation of the important Second Council of Orange in 529. The synod promulgated this decision:

> According to Catholic faith we also believe that after grace has been received through baptism, all the baptized, if they are willing to labor faithfully, can and ought to accomplish with Christ's help and cooperation what pertains to the salvation of their souls. We do not believe that some are predestined to evil by the divine power; and, furthermore, if there are those who wish to believe in such an enormity, with great abhorrence we anathematize them. We also believe and profess for our salvation that in every good work it is not that we make a beginning and afterwards are helped through God's mercy, but rather, that without any previous good merits on our part, God himself first inspires us with faith in him and love of him so that we may faithfully seek the sacrament of baptism, and so that after baptism, with his help, we may be able to accomplish what is pleasing to him. Therefore, we evidently must believe that the remarkable faith of the thief whom the Lord called to his home in paradise (Luke 23:43), the faith of Cornelius the centurion to whom an angel of the Lord was sent (Acts 10:3), and the faith of Zacchaeus who merited to receive the Lord himself (Luke 19:6), was not a gift of nature but a gift of God's generosity.[17]

We thus may observe that the Council of Orange upheld that the *initium fidei* rests with God alone, that justification is a gratuitous gift of God, that after regeneration through Baptism we cooperate with God's grace for salvation, and that it rejects as truly abhorrent a divine predestination to evil. This local council in Gaul and its ratification by Pope Boniface II[18] effectively brought to a temporary harmonious conclusion the first chapter of the debate on predestination in the West.

GREEK FATHERS AND PRE-AUGUSTINIAN LATIN FATHERS

Now that we have examined some of the Augustinian and post-Augustinian views on predestination that were to influence profoundly the subsequent history of Western Christian theology, we can now turn our attention back to the Greek fathers and the earlier Latin fathers. It appears to me that, although none of the fathers constructed an elaborate theological system to examine the mystery of predestination, there is a significant thread of unity among them. They maintained that predestination, in one way or another, involved the divine foreknowledge of human response to the gift of faith, and of the good or evil deeds that one freely chooses, thus cooperating with or rejecting the grace of God.

The particular contribution that these fathers offered us is that they presented theological, pastoral, and homiletic insights into the mystery of predestination without being confined to the formulation of the problem as addressed by the august Bishop of Hippo in his rejection of the heresy of Pelagianism. As the course of Western theology has clearly manifested itself, the juxtaposition of divine will and predestination with human free choice and moral responsibility has occasionally led to two extremes—either Pelagianism or predestinationism.

The early fathers, in their preaching and presentation of the gospel to the world, stressed the freedom of the human will to respond to the message of Jesus Christ and to turn away from Stoic determinism and astral fatalism, which were popular philosophical misconceptions that the church had to confront in the Hellenistic world. Thus, in his First Apology, Saint Justin Martyr affirmed that God foreknows (προγινώσκει) that certain men, who are not yet born, will carry out their salvation by penance.[19]

Saint Irenaeus of Lyons believed that divine predestination was conditioned by human merits preknown by God, and thus expressed himself:

> God, who foresaw all things, has prepared for each a worthy dwelling; to those who follow the pure light and tend towards it, He has prepared this light in abundance, but to those who turn themselves away and flee from it and who blind themselves in any way from it, He has prepared corresponding darkness, and He inflicts on them the pain which they have merited.[20]

Theodoret of Cyr, commenting on the famous predestination text of Rom. 8:30, observed that the predestined "are those whose inclinations, whose resolves have been foreseen, who have been predestined from on high, and predestined, they have been called."[21]

Saint Ambrose of Milan offered his commentary on Rom. 8:29, and he indicated that predestination follows foreknowledge of human merits: "He did not predestine them before He foreknew them, but He did predestine the rewards of those whose merits He foreknew."[22]

The blessed Jerome expressed himself in like manner on Rom. 8:29-30, that God did not simply predestine humans, but he predestined them in virtue of his foreknowledge: "Those whom God knew should be conformed to His Son in this life are those whom He has predestined to be conformed to Him in His glory."[23]

Elsewhere Jerome rebuked Marcion and "all the heretical dogs who mutilate the Old Testament" by insisting that the foreknowledge of God was not the cause of evil:

> He does not make use of His foreknowledge to condemn a man, though He knows that hereafter he will displease Him; but such is His goodness and unspeakable mercy that He chooses a man, who, He perceives, will meanwhile be good, and who, He knows, will turn out badly, thus giving him the opportunity of being converted and repenting. . . . For Adam did not sin because God knew that he would do so; but God, inasmuch as He is God, foreknew what Adam would do of his own free choice.[24]

Saint Hilary of Poitiers spoke about the justice of God, that divine election is not the result of an indifferent judgment on God's part, but there is a difference based on the evaluation of merits: "Those whom He has seen in advance, those also He has predestined."[25]

In commenting on the predestination passage in Ephesians, Saint John Chrysostom spoke about the conditional character of God's call and grace; he distinguished between two wills or desires in God: "The first will is that those who have sinned shall not perish, the second will is that they perish who have lived sinfully."[26] In the same section of his commentary on Ephesians, Saint Chrysostom delicately balanced divine predilection with foreknowledge of human deeds: "God has predestined us, not only by love but also by our own virtue; for if this depends only on love, all ought to be saved (for God loves all men); but if this depends on nothing other than virtue, then the coming of Jesus would be an irrelevance."[27]

In his commentary on Matthew, Saint Chrysostom spoke in the name of the heavenly judge (Matt. 25:34-44) and implied the dependence of predestination on foreknowledge: "Before you existed, all this has been prepared and arranged by Me, for I knew that you would be such (i.e., good or wicked)."[28]

In his famous homily sixteen on Romans 9, Saint Chrysostom addressed at length the difficult question why God says "Jacob I have loved, but Esau I have hated":

> What was the cause then why one was loved and the other hated? Why was it that one served, the other was served? It was because one was wicked and the other good. And yet the children being not yet born, one was honored and the other condemned. For when they were not as yet born, God said, "the elder shall serve the younger." With what intent then did God say this? Because He doth not wait, as man doth, to see from the issue of their acts the good and him who is not so, but even before these He knoweth which is the wicked and which is not such. . . . And He shows that noble birth after the flesh is of no avail, but we must seek for virtue of soul, but even before the works of it God knoweth. For "the children," he says, "being not yet born, nor having done any good or evil, that the purpose of God according to election might stand, it was said unto her that the elder shall serve the younger": for this was a sign of foreknowledge, that they were chosen from the very birth. That the election made according to foreknowledge might be manifestly of God, from the first day He

at once saw and proclaimed which was good and which was not.[29]

In his treatise *On the Orthodox Faith*, Saint John of Damascus (c.675–c.749), who wrote considerably later than the fathers we have so far investigated, purposefully intended not to introduce any innovations but to express faithfully the received tradition of the church in Sacred Scripture and in the fathers. When he addressed the question of predestination, he reproduced the consensus of the patristic commentaries and supported the position that predestination is based upon divine foreknowledge and that God does not will the sin or the reprobation of sinners:

> One should also bear in mind that God antecedently wills all to be saved and to attain to His kingdom. For He did not form us to be chastised, but, because He is good, that we might share in His goodness. Yet, because He is just, He does wish to punish sinners. So the first is called *antecedent will* and *approval*, and it has Him as its cause; the second is called *consequent will* and *permission*, and it has ourselves as its cause. This last is twofold: that which is by dispensation and for our instruction and salvation, and that which is abandonment to absolute chastisement, as we have said. These, however, belong to those things which do not depend upon us.
>
> As to the things which do depend upon us, the good ones He wills antecedently and approves, whereas the evil, which are essentially bad, He neither wills antecedently nor consequently, but permits them to the free will. . . .
>
> One should note that God foreknows all things but that He does not predestine them all. Thus He foreknows the things that depend on us, but He does not predestine them—because neither does He will evil to be done nor does He force virtue. And so, predestination is the result of the divine command made with foreknowledge. Those things which do not depend on us, however, He predestines in accordance with His foreknowledge. For, through His foreknowledge, He has already decided all things beforehand in accordance with His goodness and justice.[30]

These representative observations from the Greek and Latin Fathers present us with a consensus from tradition that predestination involves the divine foreknowledge of man's good or evil deeds. Saint Augustine, however, in his attempt to safeguard the mystery of salvation from the heresy of Pelagianism, taught a more extreme position on predestination, one which charted the course for later medieval and Reformation debates on the topic. Within this context, the views of this splendid teacher should not be received unqualifiedly or be seen in isolation from the other doctors of the universal Church.

As far as the later Orthodox Church is concerned, there is no explicit doctrinal definition or teaching concerning predestination and related questions, other than the acceptance of the patristic consensus. When, during the course of the seventeenth century, the Orthodox Church was confronted with the new perspectives of the Protestant Reformation, several statements of faith appeared and local synods addressed these sundry issues.[31] These creeds do not enjoy the authority of the decrees of the early ecumenical councils, but they are representative of the response of the living Church Tradition when confronted with questions about the faith in a given situation.

The final word can never be said about the mystery of predestination. However, the subsequent debates in the Western Church concerning predestination should be evaluated within the context of the fullness of the patristic tradition.

Notes

Introduction: Lutheran–Orthodox Dialogue in North America

1. Minutes of the Agenda Committee for Lutheran–Orthodox Conversations, December 10, 1965.
2. Archbishop Iakovos, consultations with Pres. George Harkins and Dr. Paul Empie, National Lutheran Council, May 6, 1965.
3. Papers by R. Tobias and J. Travis in vol. 2 of the dialogue reports.
4. Papers by J. Jorgenson and R. Tobias in vol. 2.
5. Crete statement, *Orthodox Contributions to Nairobi* (Geneva: World Council of Churches, 1976), 25–33.
6. Papers by S. Harakas, J. Meyendorff, P. Rorem, C. Volz, R. Wilken, vol. 2.
7. Papers by S. Harakas, J. Breck, R. Wilken, vol. 2.
8. Papers by J. Breck, S. Harakas, P. Rorem, vol. 2.

Common Statement: Christ "In Us" and Christ "For Us" in Lutheran and Orthodox Theology

1. An English translation of Cyril's letter to John can be found in T. Herbert Bindley, *The Oecumenical Documents of the Faith* (London: (Methuen & Co.), 1925), 272–78.
2. See Ernst Benz, *Wittenberg und Byzanz*. Zur Begegnung und Auseinandersetzung der Reformation und der oestlich-orthodoxen Kirche (Marburg: (N. G. Elwert Verlag), 1949), 114. The translation of the Latin *justificari* is not consistent. At a number of places it is rendered by terms formed from the root *dikaios*, at least in the 1730 edition. See *Augustana Confessio Germanica et Latina cum versione Graeca Pauli Dolsci* ed. M. C. Reineccius (Leipzig: 1730). On this point see Wayne James Jorgenson, "The Augustana Graeca and the Correspondence Between the Tübingen Lutherans and Patriarch Jeremias: Scripture and Tradition in Theological Methodology" (University Microfilms, Dissertation, Boston University, 1979).
3. See Bishop Maximos Aghiorgoussis, "Orthodox Soteriology," [in this volume].

171

4. Bishop Kallistos Ware's remark occurs in the foreword to Georgios I. Mantzaridis, *The Deification of Man* (Crestwood, NY: St. Vladimir's Press, 1984), 7.

5. For the theological significance of "energies" in Orthodox theology, see Christos Yannaras, "The Distinction Between Essence and Energies and Its Importance for Theology," *Saint Vladimir's Theological Quarterly* 19 (1975): 232–45.

6. Vladimir Lossky, *In the Image and Likeness of God* (Crestwood, NY: Saint Vladimir's Press, 1958), 98.

7. "Lectures on Galatians 1535," in American Edition of *Luther's Works*, vol. 26 trans. Jaroslav Pelikan (Saint Louis: Concordia Publishing House, 1963), 287.

8. Apology to the Augsburg Confession (Ap) 4.43 in *The Book of Concord (BC)* ed. Theodore G. Tappert (Philadelphia: Fortress Press, 1959), 113.

9. "Sermons on the Second Epistle of Saint Peter" at 1.4, in American Edition of *Luther's Works, The Catholic Epistles*, trans. Margin H. Bertram (Saint Louis: Concordia Publishing House, 1967), 155.

10. Johann Arndt, *True Christianity*, introduction and trans. Peter Erb (New York: Paulist Press, 1979), 45–46. It is significant that Arndt's writings were popular with leading representatives of Orthodox spirituality, e.g., Saint Tikhon of Zadonsk. cf. Elisabeth Behrsigel "Hesychasm and the Western Impact in Russia: St. Tikhon of Zadonsk (1724–1783)" in Lonis Dupré and Don E. Saliers, eds., in cooperation with John Meyehdorff, *Christian Spirituality III Post-Reformation and Modern* (New York: Crossroads, 1989), pp. 432–445.

11. Formula of Concord (FC) 8.34, *BC*, 597.

12. For a discussion of patristic ideas of *theosis* from the perspective of the Reformation debates, see William Rusch, "How the Eastern Fathers Understood what the Western Meant by Justification" in *Justification by Faith: Lutherans and Catholics in Dialogue VII* (Minneapolis: Augsburg, 1985), 131–42. See also Henry Edwards, "Justification, Sanctification and the Eastern Orthodox Concept of 'Theosis' " in *Consensus: A Canadian Lutheran Journal of Theology* 14 (1988): 65–80. G. L. Bray, "Justification and the Eastern Orthodox Churches" in *Here We Stand: Justification by Faith Today*, ed. David Field (London: Hodder and Stoughton, 1986), 103–19.

13. Gregory of Nyssa, "in Gregorii Nysseni Opera, Contra Eunomium Libri, (2.91), vol. 1, ed. Werner Jaeger (Leiden: E. J. Brill, 1960), 253.

14. *Dialogue Between Neighbours: The Theological Conversations Between the Evangelical-Lutheran Church of Finland and the Russian Orthodox Church 1970–1986*, ed. Hannu T. Kamppuri, *Publication of the Luther-Agricola Society*, B 17 (Helsinki, 1986): 19. [Bill Rusch will add the item on the Finnish dialogue on Luther and *Theosis*.]

15. Lossky, *In the Image*, 99–100.

16. "Athanasius, Contra Gentes and De Incarnatione, ed. Robert W. Thompson (Oxford: Clarendon Press, 1971), 183.

17. John Meyendorff, *Byzantine Theology* (New York: Fordham University Press, 1979), 160.

18. "Christ Jesus Lay in Death's Strong Bands" (Christ Lag in Todesbanden), *The Lutheran Book of Worship* (Minneapolis: Augsburg, 1978), no. 134.

19. Gregory of Nyssa, "De Hominis Opificio 16." *Patrologia graeca* 44 (1846) col. 184 B.

20. *Basilii Caesareae Cappadocini Opera Omnia*, ed. Julien Garnier (Paris, 1839), vol. 2, 445.

21. John Gerhard, *Locorum Theologicorum*. Tomus Quartus, ed. J. F. Cotta (Tübingen, 1765). Locus IX, *De Imagine Dei in Homine ante Lapsum* can be found on pages 237–93. The relevant passage is on page 289ff. (9.10.38).

22. "Contra Eunomium Libri," (3.10). vol. 2, 293.
23. Epitome 1 on Original Sin, Thesis 1 FC *BC*, 466.
24. "Ground and Reason of Articles Unjustly Condemned" (Weimar Ausgabe, vol. 7, 445).
25. See Robert L. Wilken, "Justification by Works: Fate and the Gospel in the Roman Empire," *Concordia Theological Monthly*, 40 (1969), 379–92.
26. Kallistos Ware, *The Orthodox Way* (Crestwood, NY: St. Vladimir's Press, 1979), 75–6.
27. John Chrysostom, "Homilies on Matthew," 82.4 (*Patrologia graeca* 57, col. 742).
28. "Epitome 2 on Free Will, Antithesis 9" *BC*, 466.
29. "Saint Gregory, Patriarch of Constantinople, Theological Orations," 4.6 *Christology of the Later Fathers*, ed. E. B. Hardy and Cyril Richardson (Philadelphia: The Westminster Press, 1954), 181.

Chapter 1: Orthodox Soteriology

1. John H. Leith, *Creeds of the Churches* (New York: Anchor Books, 1963), 33.
2. Maximos Aghiorgoussis, "The Dogmatic Tradition of the Orthodox Church," in *A Companion to the Greek Orthodox Church* (New York: Greek Orthodox Archdiocese, 1984), 160–1.
3. Aghiorgoussis, "The Dogmatic Tradition," 161–2.
4. Aghiorgoussis, "The Dogmatic Tradition," 162–4.
5. John Meyendorff, *Byzantine Theology* (New York: Fordham University Press, 1974), 151–2.
6. Constantine Dratsellas, "Questions of the Soteriological Teaching of the Greek Fathers" Athens (reprinted from *Theologia*) 1969, 9–10.
7. See Dratsellas, "Questions," 58–64; Meyendorff, *Byzantine Theology*, 159ff.
8. Aghiorgoussis, "The Dogmatic Tradition," 164.
9. John Meyendorff, *Byzantine Theology*, 160–1.
10. Aghiorgoussis, "The Dogmatic Tradition," 164–5.
11. Aghiorgoussis, "The Dogmatic Tradition," 165.
12. See Dratsellas, "Questions," 98–103.
13. Dratsellas, "Questions," 98.
14. Dratsellas, "Questions," 101–2.
15. Dratsellas, "Questions," 103.
16. Dratsellas, "Questions," 104–5.
17. Dratsellas, "Questions," 106–10.
18. Aghiorgoussis, "The Dogmatic Tradition," 165–6.
19. Dratsellas, "Questions," 114.
20. Aghiorgoussis, "The Dogmatic Tradition," 166.
21. See Meyendorff, *Byzantine Theology*, 173–6.
22. Dratsellas, "Questions," 123.
23. Aghiorgoussis, "The Dogmatic Tradition," 166–8.
24. Meyendorff, *Byzantine Theology*, 146.

Chapter 2: Humanity: "Old" and "New"—Anthropological Considerations

1. Athanasius, *On the Incarnation*, 54. *Patrologia graeca* 25, vol. 192B.
2. Hannu T. Kamppuri, *Methekis* (Helsinki: Suomalaisen Teologisen Kirjallisuusseuran tulkaisuja, 157, 1988).

3. John Meyendorff, "Creation in the History of Orthodox Theology," *Saint Vladimir's Theological Quarterly* 27 vol. 1 (1983): 27–37.

4. J. Pain and N. Zernov, *A Bulgakov Anthology* (Philadelphia: Westminster Press, 1976), 152.

5. See my study "Christ's Humanity: The Paschal Mystery" in *St. Vladimir's Theological Quarterly*, 31 (1987), 1, pp. 5–40.

Chapter 3: Salvation as Justification and *Theosis*

1. Carl E. Braaten, *Principles of Lutheran Theology* (Philadelphia: Fortress Press, 1983), 63.

2. J. N. D. Kelly, *Early Christian Creeds* (New York: Longmans, 1972), 296.

3. Emilianos Timiadis, *The Nicene Creed: Our Common Faith* (Philadelphia: Fortress Press, 1983), 19, 36.

4. For "A Lutheran View of the Council of Nicaea 325 AD," see the position paper for the Lutheran–Orthodox Dialogue in North America by Carl Andrew Volz, December 10–11, 1984, vol. 2 of the Dialogue reports.

5. The basic Lutheran confessions of the sixteenth century are published in a critical edition of the original German and Latin texts, edited by Hans Lietzmann, et al., as *Die Bekenntnisschriften der evangelisch-lutherischen Kirche*, 6, durchgesehene Auflage (Göttingen: Vandenhoeck & Ruprecht, 1967). It is available in English (based on the second German edition of 1952) as *The Book of Concord: The Confessions of the Evangelical Lutheran Church*, trans. and ed. Theodore G. Tappert, et al. (Philadelphia: Fortress Press, 1959).

   While Lutherans regard the Holy Scriptures as the sole norm for the faith and life of the church, they are united in the conviction that the documents in *The Book of Concord (BC)* are true witnesses to the gospel which grasp and succinctly set forth the essentials of the Bible. Published on July 25, 1580, it includes (in addition to the three ecumenical creeds of the early church) the Augsburg Confession (AC, or *CA = Confessio Augustana*), which is universally regarded as the basic expression of the faith confessed by all Lutherans, and the Small Catechism (SC), which has enjoyed the most widespread usage. The remainder has often been treated as commentary: Large Catechism (LC), Apology of the Augsburg Confession (Ap), Smalcald Articles (SA), Treatise on the Power and Primacy of the Pope (TrP), and Formula of Concord (FC).

6. In *Justification by Faith: Lutherans and Catholics in Dialogue VII*, ed. Anderson, H. George, T. Austin Murphy, and Joseph A. Burgess (Minneapolis: Augsburg, 1985), 168.

7. William G. Rusch, "How the Eastern Fathers Understood What the Western Church Meant by Justification," in *Justification by Faith*, 131.

8. Braaten, *Principles*, 63.

9. Eric W. Gritsch and Robert W. Jenson, *Lutheranism: The Theological Movement and Its Confessional Writings* (Philadelphia: Fortress Press, 1976), 36.

10. Bernhard Lohse, *A Short History of Christian Doctrine*, trans. F. Ernest Stoeffler (Philadelphia: Fortress Press, 1966), 169.

11. Timothy Ware (Archimandrite Kallistos), *The Orthodox Church*, rev. ed., (New York: Penguin Books, 1980), 29.

12. *Against the Roman Papacy*, Weimarer Ausgabe (WA) LIV, 285; LW XLI, 359. Cf. also *The Freedom of A Christian*, WA VII, 22; LW XXI, 346.

13. Although it is usually the Augsburg Confession and the other Lutheran Confessions which are normative for Lutherans in interconfessional dialogue, some of those Confessions are written by Luther and the others often invoke his writings and honor them as insights into the Word of God. To omit the writings of Luther would be to ignore not only much that is formative of contemporary Lutheran thinking but "a theology which, in depth and integrity, is perhaps without equal in the history of the church and in the history of dogma," Bernhard Lohse, *A Short History of Christian Doctrine*, trans. F. Ernest Stoeffler (Philadelphia: Fortress Press, 1966), 184. After all, as Paul Tillich opines, "Lutheranism is something which historically has been associated with Protestant Orthodoxy, political movements, Prussian conservatism, and what not. But Luther is different. He is one of the few great prophets of the Christian Church, and his greatness is overwhelming," *A History of Christian Thought*, ed. Carl E. Braaten (New York: Harper & Row, 1968), 227.

Nothing approaching a complete critical edition of Luther's writings was available until the "Weimar Edition" began to appear in the late nineteenth century (*Weimarer Ausgabe*—hence the familiar *WA* abbreviation). Still in process, the edition already numbers 102 large books, published in four sets: (1) *Werke* (general works, arranged chronologically by type of work in 58 volumes numbering 70 separately bound books to date. Several volumes are subdivided into two or three separately bound sections [*Abteilungen*]. The first *Abteilung* of vol. 10, is divided into "halves"; hence the standard reference form, e.g.: "*WA* X.1.II, 218" which indicates "page 218 of the second half of the first section of volume ten"); (2) *Tischreden* [*WA,TR*] (Table Talk, complete in six volumes, 1912–1921); (3) *Die Deutsche Bibel* [*WA,DB*] (12 volumes, numbering 15 books to date, 1906–); and (4) *Briefe* [*WA,Br*] (letters, 11 volumes to date and complete with the exception of an index volume, 1930–).

Including a large selection from all four sets of the *WA* is the "American Edition" of *Luther's Works*, ed. Jaroslav Pelikan and Helmut T. Lehman, 55 volumes (Philadelphia: Fortress Press, and Saint Louis: Concordia Publishing House, 1955–1987) [abbreviated *LW*]. All references to English translations are given following the *WA* reference, separated by a semicolon.

14. Sermons on the Gospel of John, *WA* XLVII, 92; *LW* XXII, 368.

15. Eight Sermons at Wittenberg, *WA* XIII, 55; *LW* LI, 95.

16. "Sermon on the Sum of the Christian Life," *WA* XXXVI, 360; *LW* LI, 269. Cf. also *Heidelberg Disputation, WA* I, 365; *LW* XXXI, 57.

17. *Lectures on Galatians, WA* XL.1, 462; *LW* XXVI, 298.

18. Works on the First Twenty-Two Psalms, *WA* V, 38; *LW* XIV, 300.

19. Joseph A. Sittler, *The Doctrine of the Word in the Structure of Lutheran Theology* (Philadelphia: Muhlenberg Press, 1948), 15.

20. Sermons on the Gospel of John, *WA* XLVII, 94; *LW* XXII, 371. See also, Weekly Sermons on John 16–20, *WA* XXVIII, 91.

21. *The Sacrament of the Body and Blood of Christ—Against the Fanatics, WA* XIX, 492; *LW* XXXVI, 342.

22. *Lectures on Genesis, WA* XLII, 625; *LW* III, 108.

23. *Lectures on Genesis, WA* XLIII, 71–72; *LW* III, 275. The presence of the sacraments in this list makes it clear that Luther did not simplistically identify "the Word" with human words of any sort.

24. *Lectures on Genesis, WA* XLII, 296; *LW* II, 49. Luther's own experience supported his conviction that God takes the initiative.

25. Sittler, *The Doctrine*, 16, n. 4.
26. *The Magnificat*, WA VII, 546; LW XXI, 299.
27. *Heidelberg Disputation*, WA I,354; LW XXI, 52. The bracketed words have been substituted for the puzzling translation in *LW* of *quae facta sunt* as "which have actually happened."
28. Apology, IV, par. 285 BC, 150.
29. Werner Elert, *Law and Gospel*, trans. Edward H. Schroeder (Philadelphia: Fortress Press, 1967), 11.
30. FC, Solid Declaration 6:1. See also SD 5:18 & 20 and 6:9 & 20, as well as Epitome 6:3 and 6:8.
31. Braaten, *Principles*, 112–3.
32. Luther's insights were not without impressive antecedents in the fathers of the church. However, the faith of the fathers was not living still in the understanding and practice of the church.
33. Cf. A. C. McGiffert, *Protestant Thought Before Kant* (New York: Harper & Brothers, Harper Torchbooks, 1962), 27–28.
34. "All creation is the most beautiful book or Bible; in it God has described and portrayed Himself" (Marginal Notes in Books and Bibles, WA XLVIII, 201 [my translation]).
35. LC II, 26.
36. SC II, 4.
37. WA XL.1, 371.
38. "Preface to the Complete Edition of Luther's Latin Writings," WA LIV, 186–7; LW XXXIV, 337.
39. *Defense and Explanation of all the Articles of Dr. Martin Luther which were Unjustly Condemned by the Roman Bull*, WA VII, 445; LW XXXII, 91. Cf. *The Bondage of the Will*, WA XVIII, 771; LW XXXIII, 270–1.
40. Gospel for the Sixth Sunday after Trinity, WA LII, 406 [my translation].
41. SA III, xiii, 1–2.
42. Cf. *Lectures on Isaiah*, WA XXXI.2, 439, and *The Seven Penitential Psalms* WA XVIII, 520; LW XIV, 193–94.
43. *Lectures on Galatians* (1519), WA II, 503 [my translation]; LW XXVII, 240–41.
44. *Die Promotionsdisputation von Palladius und Tilemann*, WA XXXIX.1, 205 [my translation].
45. SA, Part II, Article I.
46. *The Freedom of a Christian*, WA VII; LW XXXI, 351. Since Luther could have derived the concept from the Christmas liturgy, it is not known if he was aware of its use by the fathers in connection with divinization.
47. *Lectures on Galatians* (1535), WA XL.1, 589; LW XXVI, 387.
48. Braaten, *Principles*, 113.
49. *Disputation on Matthew* 22:1-14, WA XXXIX.1, 283.
50. WA,Br. V, 500.
51. *The Freedom of a Christian*, WA VII, 21–22; LW XXI, 344.
52. *Defense and Explanation of All the Articles*, WA VII, 337; LW XXXII, 24.
53. Vladimir Lossky, *The Mystical Theology of the Eastern Church* (Crestwood, NY: Saint Vladimir's Seminary Press, 1976), 155.
54. John Meyendorff, *Christ in Eastern Christian Thought* (Crestwood, NY: Saint Vladimir's Seminary Press, 1975), 210.
55. Lars Thunberg, *Man and the Cosmos: The Vision of Saint Maximus the Confessor* (Crestwood, NY: Saint Vladimir's Seminary Press, 1985), 51.

56. Georgios I. Mantzaridis, *The Deification of Man: Saint Gregory Palamas and the Orthodox Tradition,* trans. Liadain Sherrard (Crestwood, NY: Saint Vladimir's Seminary Press, 1984), 121.

57. Tuomo Mannermaa, *Der im Glauben gegenwaertige Christus: Rechtfertigung und Vergöttung zum oekumenischen Dialog* (Hannover: Lutherisches Verlagshaus, 1989), 99 [my translation].

58. Mantzaridis, *The Deification of Man,* 128.

59. See Ware, *The Orthodox Church,* 240-41, for his six-point description of the concept of *theosis*—which includes the assumption that repentance for sin will be a continuing act for the Christian.

60. Marc Lienhard, *Luther: Witness to Jesus Christ,* trans. Edwin H. Robertson (Minneapolis: Augsburg, 1982), 123–24. Cf. Thunberg, *Man and the Cosmos,* 131.

61. Lossky, *The Mystical Theology,* 196.

62. Meyendorff, *Christ in Eastern Christian Thought,* 210.

63. N.B: These lectures provide both the primary source for the doctrine of justification in Luther's writings and the most dramatic evidence of Luther's understanding of and contribution to the doctrine of *theosis*.

64. *Lectures on Galatians* (1535), *WA* XL.I, 228–9; *LW* XXVI, 129–30. See also *LW* XXVI, 430–1, where Luther shows that it is the formation of Christ in us, by faith, that restores the image and likeness of God.

65. Eric W. Gritsch, "The Origins of the Lutheran Teaching on Justification," in *Justification by Faith: Lutherans and Catholics in Dialogue VII,* ed. Anderson, H. George, T. Austin Murphy, and Joseph A. Burgess (Minneapolis: Augsburg, 1985), 166.

66. Heinrich Bornkamm, *Luther's World of Thought,* trans. Martin H. Bertram (St. Louis: Concordia Publishing House, 1958), 171.

67. Ap. IV, 194 and 365–9 (BC, 133, 163).

68. AC VI (BC, 31).

69. Meyendorff, *Christ in Eastern Christian Thought,* 211.

70. Vladimir Lossky, *The Vision of God,* 2d ed., trans. Asheleigh Moorhouse (Leighton Buzzard, England: The Faith Press, 1973), 81. Luther also used the image of the fire in the blacksmith's iron (cf. *LW* XXIII, 123).

71. *Lectures on Galatians* (1535), *WA* XL.I, 282; *LW* XXVI, 167.

72. *Lectures on Galatians* (1535), *WA* XL.I, 182, 390; *LW* XXVI, 100, 247.

73. Gregory Palamas, *Defense of the Hesychasts,* quoted in Mantzaridis, *The Deification of Man,* 124.

74. Ware, *The Orthodox Church,* 227.

75. Ware, *The Orthodox Church,* 230.

76. Quoted by Jaroslav Pelikan, *The Christian Tradition: A History of the Development of Doctrine,* vol. 2: *The Spirit of Eastern Christendom* (Chicago: University of Chicago Press, 1974), 182.

77. Pelikan, *The Christian Tradition,* 182.

Chapter 4: Human Participation in the Divine/Human Dialogue

1. Edmund Schlink, *Theology of the Lutheran Confessions,* trans. Herbert J. A. Bouman (Philadelphia: Muhlenberg Press, 1961), 38.

2. Martin Luther, Large Catechism (LC) II:16, in *The Book of Concord,* ed. Theodore G. Tappert (Philadelphia: Muhlenberg Press, 1959), 412. Hereafter *The Book of Concord* will be referred to as *BC*.

3. Paul Sponheim, "Sin and Evil," in *Christian Dogmatics*, ed. Carl Braaten and Robert Jenson (Philadelphia: Fortress Press, 1984), I:382.

4. Formula of Concord (FC), "Epitome," XI:2, *BC*, 492:2. Sponheim, *op. cit.*, "In any case, Christian reflection concerning the demonic does not challenge, but rather supports and strengthens, our understanding of sin as will against will. It is will against God, as Article XI of the Formula puts it; "Everything which prepares and fits man through sin, and in no way from God."

5. Luther, LC, *BC*, 414:28.

6. Jaroslav Pelikan, *The Emergence of the Catholic Tradition* (Chicago: University of Chicago Press, 1971), 318.

7. Augsburg Confession (AC) II, *BC*, 29.

8. Cyprian, *Epistle 64:5* (CSEL Vienna, 1857: 3:720–21).

9. Augustine, *Against Two Letters of the Pelagians* 4:12:32 (CSEL, Vienna, 1857: 60:568).

10. Origen, *Commentary on the Epistle to the Romans* 5:9. (Patrologia cursus complets, series latina, ed. J. P. Migne, Paris 1895, Vol. 14).

11. Sponheim, "Sin and Evil," 377–8.

12. Walther Eichrodt, *Theology of The Old Testament*, trans. J. A. Baker (Philadelphia: Westminster Press, 1961–1967), 2:407.

13. Gerhard von Rad, *Old Testament Theology*, trans. D. M. G. Stalker (New York: Harper and Row, 1962–1965), 2:394.

14. Schlink, *Theology of the Lutheran Confessions*, 41.

15. Augustine, *Epistle 166:7*, 10, 16, 18, 20, 25.

16. Luther, *Disputation Against the Scholastics* (1517), WA 1:225.

17. Luther, LC, BC, 16/17:366/367.

18. FC, "Solid Declaration," 1:11, *BC*, 510.

19. FC, "Solid Declaration," 1, *BC*, 510:10: "Luther's understanding of the image of God is this: 'that Adam had it in his being and that he not only was wholly godly; that is, he was without the fear of death or of any other danger, and was content with God's favor.' All of that was lost and would be fully restored only after Judgement Day. In its place had come death and the fear of death, blasphemy, hatred toward God, and lust: 'These and similar evils are the image of the devil, who stamped them on us.' " Jaroslav Pelikan, *Reformation of Church and Dogma* (1300–1700) (Chicago: University of Chicago Press, 1984), 142.

20. Ap IV, BC 161:351.

21. Ap II, BC 102:14.

22. *Time*, 21 March 1969, p. 62.

23. *The Lutheran Book of Worship*, 121. (Augsburg Publishing House, Mineapolis, 1978).

24. *The Lutheran Book of Worship*, 122. (Augsburg Publishing House, Mineapolis, 1978).

25. FC, "Solid Declaration," I, *BC*, 519:61.

26. FC, "Epitome," I, *BC*, 466:2. Clearly one's definition of human nature is crucial, as it impinges upon one's Christology and the nature of the humanity which Christ assumed.

27. FC, "Solid Declaration," I BC, 514:34.

28. Luther, *Ground and Reason of Articles Unjustly Condemned*, WA 7:445.

29. Luther, *Exposition on Genesis* 2:7, WA 42:64.

30. Ap XVIII, *BC*, 225:4.

31. AC XVIII, *BC*, 39:2.

32. Werner Elert, *The Christian Ethos*, trans. Carl J. Schindler (Philadelphia: Muhlenberg Press, 1957), 144.
33. Irenaeus, *Against Heresies* 4:37:3 (Sancti Irenaei, episcopi lugenensis, ed. W. Wigan Harvey, Cambridge, 1857).
34. Robert Jenson, "Pneumatological Soteriology," *Christian Dogmatics* 11:128. (Ed. Braaten and Jenson, Fortress Press, Philadelphia, 1984).
35. Ap IV, *BC*, 108:5.
36. Ap IV, *BC*, 133:43.
37. Ap IV, *BC*, 113:42,43.
38. Ronald F. Thiemann, *Revelation and Theology: The Gospel as Narrative Promise* (Notre Dame: University of Notre Dame Press, 1985), 99. I am in debt to Thiemann for the concepts of prevenience expressed here.
39. Ap IV, *BC*, 113:48.
40. Ap IV, *BC*, 113:48.
41. Cited by Schlink, *Theology of the Lutheran Confessions*, 96.
42. AC XX, *BC*, 44-45:26-25.
43. AC, *BC*, 30:3.
44. Ap IV, *BC*, 119:86.
45. *The Lutheran Book of Worship*, 56, (Augsburg Publishing House, Mineapolis, 1978). A similar emphasis is found in the absolution of the Episcopalian rite: "Almighty God have mercy on you, forgive you all your sins through our Lord Jesus Christ, strengthen you in all goodness, and by the power of the Holy Spirit keep you in eternal life." *Book of Common Prayer*, 360.
46. Luther, *Preface to Romans*, *LW*, 35:370.
47. Gerhard Forde, "Christian Life," *Christian Dogmatics* II:439.
48. Forde, "Christian Life," 439–40.
49. Luther, *WA* 10:1, 2:4:31. 6ff.
50. Luther, *WA*.
51. AC XX, *BC*, 45:27. Cf. Gustaf Wingren, *Luther on Vocation* (Philadelphia: Muhlenberg Press, 1957).
52. Luther, "Freedom of a Christian," in *Three Treatises* (Philadelphia: Fortress Press, 1966), 277.
53. Luther, "Freedom of a Christian," 294.
54. Ap IV, *BC*, 133:194.
55. Forde, "Christian Life," 437, referring to Wilfried Joest, Gesetz und Freiheit.
56. Forde, "Christian Life," 402–3.
57. AC XIII, *BC*, 35:1.
58. Ap XIII, *BC*, 21:5.
59. Arthur Carl Piepkorn, "The Sacred Ministry and Holy Ordination in the Symbolical Books of the Lutheran Church," *Concordia Theological Monthly*, September 1969, 552ff., argues there may be five sacraments (including Absolution, Ordination, and Marriage). The Augsburg Confession states: "(They) are not only signs by which people might be identified outwardly as Christians, but they are signs and testimonies of God's will toward us for the purpose of awakening and strengthening our faith. For this reason they require faith and they are rightly used when they are received in faith and for the purpose of strengthening faith (Art XVIII)." We read in the Apology, "No intelligent person will quibble about the number of sacraments or the terminology, so long as those things are kept which have God's command and promise." Ap XIII, *BC*, 213:17.

179

60. Luther, Small Catechism (SC), *BC*, 349:12. When asked why the old Adam did not remain drowned, Luther is said to have quipped it was because the old Adam was a good swimmer.

61. AC IX, *BC*, 33:1,2.

62. Luther, *On the Day of Sts. Peter and Paul*, *WA*, 52:663ff.

63. Luther, *The Blessed Sacrament of the Holy and True Body of Christ* (1519), *WA*, 2:743.

64. AC X, *BC*, 34:1, 2.

65. AC XXIV, *BC*, 56:9.

66. Ap XXIV, *BC*, 252:19.

67. Robert W. Jenson, *Visible Words* (Philadelphia: Fortress Press, 1978), 70.

68. *The Lutheran Book of Worship*, 67, 68.

69. AC IX, *BC* 33:1.

70. Ap IV, *BC*, 49:310.

71. Ap IV, *BC*, 189:94.

72. Ap XII, 187:41; Apology XIII, *BC*, 211:4; LC, *BC*, 445:74.

73. AC XI, *BC*, 34:1, 2.

74. AC, *BC*, 61:1.

75. See Walter R. Bouman, "Private Confession and Absolution," *Una Sancta*, vol. XVIII, no. 2, (1961): 9–15.

Chapter 6: The Image of God in Classical Lutheran Theology

1. See H. Merki, *Homoiosis theo: Von der platonischen Angelichung an Gott zur Gott-aehnlichkeit bei Gregor von Nyssa* (Paradosis VII; Freiburg i.d. Schweiz, 1952); and R. Bernard, *L'image de Dieu d'après saint Athanase* (Théologie XXV, Paris, 1952).

2. Martin Luther, *Lectures on Genesis* in Weimar Ausgabe (*WA*), vol. 42, 45. Translation in American Edition of *Luther's Works LW* vol. 1, ed. J. Pelikan, trans. G. Schick (Philadelphia: Fortress Press, and St. Louis: Concordia Publishing House, 1955–1987), 60.

3. Citations from the *Lectures on Genesis* taken from commentary on Gen. 1:26, *WA*, vol. 42, 41–49; in *LW*, 55–65.

4. Apology to the Augsburg Confession (Ap) 2.14.

5. *Lectures on Genesis*, *WA*, vol. 42, 46.

6. Citations of Gerhard from *Locorum Theologicorum*. Tomus Quartus, ed. J. F. Cotta (Tuebingen, 1765). Locus IX, De Imagine Dei in Homine ante Lapsum can be found on pages 237–93 immediately prior to the locus on original sin. A partial (and free) translation of this section from Gerhard's dogmatics is available in *The Doctrine of Man in Classical Lutheran Theology*, ed. H. A. Preus and E. Smits (Minneapolis: Augsburg, 1962).

7. See for example Werner Elert, *Der Christliche Glaube. Grundlinien der lutherischen Dogmatik* (Hamburg: Furche-Verlag, 1956), 278–9; also Francis Pieper, *Christian Dogmatics*, vol. 1 (Saint Louis: Concordia Publishing House, 1950), 515–77. For more recent attempts to interpret the image of God, see the essay by Philip Hefner in *Christian Dogmatics* (Philadelphia: Fortress, 1984), 323–40; and Wolfhart Pannenberg, *Anthropology in Theological Perspective* (Philadelphia: Westminster, 1985), 43–79.

8. See for example the statement in the Formula of Concord, Article 1 on original sin, Solid Declaration, par. 10. "That original sin is the complete lack or absence of the original concreated righteousness of paradise or of the image of God

according to which man was originally created in truth, holiness, and righteousness, together with a disability and ineptitude as far as the things of God are concerned. As the Latin words [in the Apology] put it, 'The description of original sin denies to unrenewed human nature the gifts and the power, or the faculty and the concrete acts, to begin and to effect anything in spiritual matters.' "

Chapter 7: Election: A Lutheran–Biblical View

1. C. F. W. Walther, *Election* (Saint Charles: Holy Cross Press, 1981), 1.
2. E. Lueker, ed., *Lutheran Cyclopedia* (St. Louis: Concordia Publishing House, 1954), 839.
3. A. L. Graebner, *Outlines of Doctrinal Theology* (St. Louis: Concordia Publishing House, n.d.), 222.
4. Franz Pieper, *Christian Dogmatics* vol. 3 (St. Louis: Concordia Publishing House, 1950), 473.
5. For the material in this section I am indebted to the late Dr. Martin Scharlemann who shared this outline in a class lecture at Concordia Seminary, St. Louis. His sources, if any, were not indicated in the class notes.
6. *Luther's Works (LW)* vol. 14, ed. Jaroslav Pelikan and Helmut T. Lehmann (St. Louis: Concordia, 1960–1986), 107.
7. H. E. Jacobs, *A Summary of the Christian Faith* (Philadelphia: The United Lutheran Publication House, 1905), 553.
8. *LW* vol. 10, 1748.
9. *LW* vol. 2, 181, and vol. 8, 730.
10. *LW* vol. 3, 483.
11. *LW* vol. 18, 1795.
12. *LW* vol. 18, 1965.
13. W. Joest, *Encyclopedia of the Lutheran Church*, vol. 3 (Philadelphia: Muhlenberg Press, n.d.), 1957.
14. John Calvin, *Institutes of the Christian Religion* (3; 23, 7.)
15. J. Arminius, *Writings*, vol. 1, 221.
16. Arminius, *Writings*, 339, 355.
17. F. Schleiermacher, *The Christian Faith*, 547.
18. Schleiermacher, *The Christian Faith*, 549.
19. See Karl Barth, *Church Dogmatics* (et. Edinburgh, 1957; *Die Lehre von Gott*, Zurich, 1942), II/2 Chapter VII.
20. See Emil Brunner, *Dogmatics* vol. 1 (et. Philadelphia, 1950; *Die Christliche Lehre Von Gott*, Zurich 1946), 303f.
21. Brunner, *Dogmatics*, 305.
22. Brunner, *Dogmatics*, 338.
23. See Robert W. Jenson, "Predestination" in *Christian Dogmatics*, vol. 2 (Philadelphia: Fortress Press, 1984), 134f.
24. Jenson, "Predestination," 134.
25. Jenson, "Predestination," 136.
26. Jenson, "Predestination."
27. Jenson, "Predestination," 137.
28. Jenson, "Predestination," 138.
29. Jenson, "Predestination."
30. *LW*, vol. 10, 1764.

Chapter 8: Response to Frederick Harm's "Election: A Lutheran Biblical View"

1. E. Lueker, ed., *Lutheran Cyclopedia* (St. Louis: Concordia Publishing House, 1954), 839.
2. B. M. Metzger, *A Textual Commentary on the Greek New Testament* (New York: American Bible Society, 1975), 636f.

Chapter 9: Predestination According to Divine Foreknowledge in Patristic Tradition

1. Cf. the pertinent scholia on the terms referring to predestination in Ferdnand Prat, *The Theology of Saint Paul*, I, Westminster, MD: Newman Press, 1926, 433–7.
2. Some of the textual references are found in J. M. Rist, "Augustine on Free Will and Predestination" *Journal of Theological Studies* 20 (1969): 420-47; and in G. Bavaud, "La doctrine de la prédestination et de la reprobation d'après s. Augustin et Calvin," *Revue des études Augustiniennes* 5 (1959): 431–8.
3. "Praescientia et preparatio beneficiorum Dei, quibus certissime liberantur quicumque liberantur": *De dono perseverentiae* 14:35.
4. *De praedestinatione sanctorum* 17:41; *De dono perseverentiae* 14:35.
5. *De correptione et gratia*, 14.
6. *De gratia et libero arbitrio*, 16.
7. "In quo omnes peccaverunt"; the misreading of (ἐφ᾿ᾧ) in Romans 5:12.
8. *De correptione et gratia* 10:28: "gratia fit, gratis fit, gratiae sunt agendae quia fit."
9. *De dono perseverentiae* 9:21.
10. *In Joannem homiliae*, 26.
11. *Enchiridion* 100:26.
12. *Ad Simplicianum: epistula* 211:6, 19.
13. *De correptione et gratia* 14:44 and 15:47; *Enchiridion* 103:27.
14. K. Bihlmeyer and H. Tüchle, "Augustine's Theory of Predestination," *Church History*, vol. 1 *Christian Antiquity*, Westminster, MD: Newman Press, 1958, 285–6.
15. Bihlmeyer and Tüchle, "Augustine's Theory," 287–89.
16. *Liber responsionum*, 2.
17. Denzinger, *Enchiridion Symbolorum*, 200.
18. Denzinger, 200 a and b.
19. *Apology* 1:28. As H. D. Simonin ("La prédestination d'après lès pères grecs," DTC 12,2:2818) observes, "Justin prefers the word foreknowledge (πρόγνωσις) to the word predestination (προόρισμος), and this usage will receive its definitive consecration by John Damascene."
20. *Adversus Haereses* 4:39,4.
21. *In Rom.* 8:30; cf. also *In Eph.* 1:4 and *In Ps* 57; 58:4.
22. *De fide* 5:83.
23. *In epistulam ad Romanos* 8:29.
24. *Dialogus contra pelagianos* 3:6.
25. *In Pss* 66;67; cf. also *In Pss* 64;65.
26. *In epistulam ad Ephesios homiliae* 1:2.
27. *In epistulam ad Ephesios homiliae*.
28. *In Matthaeum, homilia* 79.
29. *In epistulam ad Romanos homiliae* 16 (translation from NPNF 11; 464–66). There is an uneasiness among some contemporary Western theologians about the

terminology and formulations of Saint John Chrysostom, often explaining these as homiletic hyperbole. Cf. A. Kenny, "Was Saint John Chrysostom a Semi-Pelagian?" *Irish Theological Quarterly* 37 (1960): 16–29, and E. Boularand, "La nécessité de la grâce pour arriver à la foi d'après Saint Jean Chrysostome," *Gregorianum* 19: 515–42.

30. *De fide orthodoxa* 3:29–30.
31. Cf. especially the Second Decree of the Council of Jerusalem (1672) concerning predestination, most handily available (although only in Greek and in a peculiar Latin translation) in Philip Schaff, *Creeds of Christendom* II (Grand Rapids, Michigan: Baker Book House, 1977), 403–5.

List of Participants

His Grace Nicholas R. Smisko of Amissos, Co-Chair
Bishop, American Carpatho-Russian Orthodox Greek Catholic Diocese in the U.S.A., Johnstown, Pennsylvania

The Very Rev. Fr. John Meyendorff, Auxiliary Co-Chair
Dean, St. Vladimir's Orthodox Theological Seminary, Crestwood, New York

The Rev. Fr. John Breck
St. Vladimir's Orthodox Theological Seminary, Crestwood, New York

His Grace Bishop Christopher (beginning 1987)
Eastern America Diocese, Serbian Orthodox Church in the U.S.A. and Canada, Edgewood Sewickley, Pennsylvania

The Rev. Fr. Stanley Harakas (through 1985)
Holy Cross Greek Orthodox School of Theology, Brookline, Massachusetts

The Rev. Fr. James Jorgenson
Sacred Heart Seminary, Detroit, Michigan

His Grace Bishop Maximos Aghiorgoussis (beginning 1989)
Greek Orthodox Archdiocese in North and South America, Pittsburgh, Pennsylvania

The Rev. Fr. John Morris
Antiochian Orthodox Church in America, Huntington, West Virginia

The Rev. Fr. Paul Schneirla (until 1984)
Antiochian Orthodox Christian Archdiocese, Brooklyn, New York
The Rev. Fr. John Travis (through 1987)
Holy Cross Greek Orthodox School of Theology, Brookline, Massachusetts
The Rev. Dr. Gregory C. Wingenbach (beginning 1987)
Director, National Department of Church and Family Life, Greek Orthodox Archdiocese in North and South America, New York, New York

ORTHODOX STAFF

His Grace Bishop Athenagoras of Dorylaion (beginning 1986)
Ecumenical Officer, Greek Orthodox Archdiocese, New York, New York
The Rev. Fr. Alexander Doumouras (through 1986, d)
Ecumenical Officer, Greek Orthodox Archdiocese, New York, New York
Ms. Elaine A. Gounaris (through 1988)
Associate Ecumenical Officer, Greek Orthodox Archdiocese, New York, New York

LUTHERAN MEMBERS

The Rev. Dr. David W. Preus, Co-Chair
Presiding Bishop, The American Lutheran Church, Minneapolis, Minnesota
The Rev. Dr. Robert Tobias, Auxiliary Co-Chair
Lutheran School of Theology at Chicago, Chicago, Illinois
The Rev. Juris Calitis
Latvian Evangelical Lutheran Church in America, Toronto, Ontario, Canada
The Rev. Dr. Frederick R. Harm
Good Shepherd Lutheran Church–Missouri Synod, Des Plaines, Illinois
The Rev. Pres. Albert M. Marcis
Ohio District, Lutheran Church–Missouri Synod, Parma, Ohio
The Rt. Rev. Michael C.D. McDaniel, Bishop
North Carolina Synod, Lutheran Church in America, Salisbury, North Carolina
The Rev. Dr. Paul E. Rorem
Lutheran School of Theology at Chicago, Chicago, Illinois

The Rev. Dr. Carl A. Volz
   Luther Northwestern Theological Seminary, St. Paul, Minnesota
The Rev. Dr. Robert L. Wilken
   University of Notre Dame, Notre Dame, Indiana

LUTHERAN STAFF

The Rev. Dr. Joseph Burgess (through 1987)
   Executive Director, Division of Theological Studies, Lutheran Council in the U.S.A., New York, New York
The Rev. Dr. Daniel F. Martensen (beginning 1988)
   Associate Director, Office for Ecumenical Affairs, Evangelical Lutheran Church in America, Chicago, Illinois
The Rev. Dr. William G. Rusch
   Executive Director, Ecumenical Relations, Lutheran Church in America, New York, New York (through 1987), and Executive Director, Office for Ecumenical Affairs, Evangelical Lutheran Church in America, Chicago, Illinois (begining 1988)